OSPREY AIRCRAFT OF THE ACES • 67

Sopwith Pup Aces of World War 1

SERIES EDITOR: TONY HOLMES

OSPREY AIRCRAFT OF THE ACES • 67

Sopwith Pup Aces of World War 1

Norman Franks

OSPREY
PUBLISHING

First published in Great Britain in 2005 by Osprey Publishing,
Midland House, West Way, Botley, Oxford OX2 0PH, UK
44-02 23rd St, Suite 219, Long Island City, NY 11101, USA
Email: info@ospreypublishing.com

Transferred to digital print on demand 2010

First published 2005
2nd impression 2008

Printed and bound by PrintOnDemand-Worldwide.com, Peterborough, UK

A CIP catalogue record for this book is available from the British Library

ISBN: 978 1 84176 886 1

Edited by Tony Holmes and Bruce Hales-Dutton
Page design by Tony Truscott
Cover Artwork by Mark Postlethwaite
Aircraft Profiles by Harry Dempsey and Scale Drawings by Mark Styling
Index by Fineline Editorial Services Ltd
Origination by PPS Grasmere Ltd, Leeds, UK

Acknowledgements

Information and photographs for this volume have come from a number of sources and from many friends. In no particular order, the
Author wishes to thank Mike O'Connor, Stuart Leslie, Les Rogers, Frank Cheesman, Andy Thomas, Tony Mellor-Ellis and Stewart
Taylor, as well as several former Pup pilots who are no longer with us. Unlike the present generation of enthusiasts, the Author and
some 'older' colleagues had the great good fortune to meet or correspond with the survivors of World War 1 who made their stories,
photos and snapshots available to them. Being all of sound mind and historically aware, they were no doubt conscious that the only
way future generations would know of their exploits, and those of dead comrades, was to entrust their memories to our care.

Front cover

By the time future seven-victory ace Capt Arthur Gould Lee claimed his first success on 4 September 1917, he was a veteran
scout pilot with many months of frontline flying to his name. Returning from a patrol over German territory at 1700 hrs in his
distinctively marked No 46 Sqn Pup B1777, he spotted a solitary RE 8 being harassed by an Albatros D III over the Polygon
Wood in eastern France. He recalled what happened next in his wartime diary;

'I've got a Hun at last! And all on my own. And confirmed. An Albatros V-Strutter, a D III. Coming back alone from a patrol,
the formation split up and we made our separate ways. It was a lovely evening, very clear, with a pale blue sky. I was gliding
down just this side of the Hun balloon lines – for once "Archie" (anti-aircraft artillery) couldn't be bothered with just one
aeroplane – when I saw an RE 8 approaching on my left front, about 500 ft below. And tracers were spitting from the
observer's gun. It was then that I realised that he was being followed, and attacked, by an Albatros V-Strutter from a range
of about 150 yards, also firing short bursts. Before I could react, the Hun ceased firing and turned east. I assumed he'd
broken off because he'd spotted me. The RE 8 whizzed past below, the observer waved, and the Albatros continued on a
level course eastwards.

'Suddenly, I woke up and dropped into a wide sweeping curve that brought me dead behind the Hun, and 200 ft above him.
It seemed incredible that he hadn't seen me when he turned aside from the RE 8. It looked so easy I suspected a trap, and
searched carefully around, but there was no other machine in sight. I came down closer and closer, holding my fire. My heart
was pounding and I was trembling uncontrollably, but my mind was calm and collected.

'I closed to within ten yards of the Hun, edged out of his slip-stream and drew nearer still until I saw that if I wasn't careful
I'd hit his rudder. His machine was green and grey and looked very spick & span. He had a dark brown flying helmet, with a
white goggle-strap round the back of his head. I aimed carefully through the Aldis between his shoulders just below where
they showed above the fairing. It was impossible to miss. I gently pressed the trigger and at the very first shots his head
jerked back. Immediately, the aeroplane reared up
vertically. He must have clutched the joy-stick right
back as he was hit. I followed upwards, still firing,
until in two or three seconds he stalled and fell over
to the left, and I had to slew sharply aside to avoid
being hit. He didn't spin, but dropped into a
near-vertical engine-on dive' (*Cover artwork by
Mark Postlethwaite*).

FOR A CATALOGUE OF ALL BOOKS PUBLISHED BY
OSPREY MILITARY AND AVIATION PLEASE CONTACT:

Osprey Direct, c/o Random House Distribution Center,
400 Hahn Road, Westminster, MD 21157
Email: uscustomerservice@ospreypublishing.com

Osprey Direct, The Book Service Ltd, Distribution Centre,
Colchester Road, Frating Green, Colchester, Essex, CO7 7DW
Email: customerservice@ospreypublishing.com

www.ospreypublishing.com

CONTENTS

A NICE LITTLE AEROPLANE

In 1988 the late aviation historian Jack Bruce described the Sopwith Pup in his own inimitable style;

'In all of aviation's ever-lengthening history, few aircraft have inspired in their pilots more affection, and fewer still have been written about with more nostalgic warmth by those who knew them, than the Sopwith Pup. Agile, responsive, docile, forgiving and, above all in its time, a doughty fighter, the Pup was a simple development of a little single-seater built in 1915 to provide Harry Hawker, the Sopwith company's test pilot, with a personal transport.

'That single-seater, the Sopwith SL TBP, with its 50 hp Gnôme rotary engine, might well have qualified to be regarded as an ultra-light by the standards of seven decades later. But with an 80 hp engine, a strengthened structure and a machine gun, its development, the Pup, was produced as a single-seat fighter in 1916. The prototype, with its Le Rhône rotary, was passed by the Sopwith experimental department on 9 February 1916. An early Royal Naval Air Service (RNAS) report on it was highly favourable, stating that "This machine is remarkable for its performance, ease of handling and for the quickness with which it can be manoeuvred".'

It is not always realised that in the early days, the Sopwith Company, with its factory and works at Kingston, in Surrey, produced aircraft mainly for the RNAS. Indeed, it was regarded as a Naval contractor, hence the report which helped push the Pup towards operational service on the Western Front in France. By the time the new scout was being sent there in the late summer of 1916, the German Air Service was also introducing new fighters such as the Halberstadt D II and DIII, the Fokker D II and the Albatros D II.

The Fokker and Albatros scouts had two machine guns rather than the Sopwith fighter's single Vickers 0.303-in weapon, and they looked a lot deadlier than the Pup. Even the name of the British scout suggested something small, warm and cuddly – it had been officially christened the Scout, but was universally known as the Pup in squadron service. The other big difference was in engine size, for the German fighters were powered by motors that produced anywhere between 100 and 160 hp.

Some of the early Royal Flying Corps (RFC) Pups were fitted with fragile Gnôme rotary engines, and

Prototype Sopwith Pup 3691 is seen at Dunkirk in the autumn of 1916. Future ace Stan Goble claimed a victory in this aircraft (the first for the Pup) on 22 September that year during the fighter's operational evaluation by 1 Naval Wing at St Pol. The prototype later served with 'Naval 3'

Pilots of 1 Naval Wing enjoy a light lunch at St Pol in the autumn of 1916. They are, from left to right (back row), F K Haskins, unknown, J H D'Albiac and unknown. In the front row, from left to right, are D C S Evill, G H Beard, 'Red' Mulock, and R S Dallas. 1 Naval Wing flew some of the first Pups to reach France

one of these was flown by William Mays Fry MC (Military Cross) upon his return to action in France with No 87 Sqn in late 1917 following a successful period with No 60 Sqn. He told the Author in 1967;

'I well remember the Pup, as I collected a few new ones for No 87 Sqn from Boulton and Paul's works at Mousehold, in Norwich. They were fitted with Gnôme rotary engines, of all unlikely things. Gnôme engines had automatic spring valve inlets in the cylinder head which were very liable to fail or break up. The petrol was vaporised in the crankcase largely by the churning up of the piston rods.

'You couldn't throttle a Gnôme down, so you controlled it by blips on a thumb switch on the joystick. The consequence was that if the engine wasn't new, or a good one, you couldn't fly level for fear of inlet valve failure or the likelihood of fire, so one progressed across country to one's destination by alternately steep climbs and then gliding down with the engine switched off. I got fed up with this one day and pushed the machine along in level flight. An inlet valve soon went and I crashed in a field near Reepham, in Norfolk. I stayed the night with a Yeomanry Regiment, which was billeted in the village, and went off to Norwich the next morning and collected a new machine in place of the crashed one. No questions were asked in those days, and we young pilots didn't worry about what happened to crashed machines, or how they were collected.

'I don't think many Pups were fitted with Gnôme engines – a good thing, as it was a dangerous aeroplane with it. The nearest thing I can remember to anything like that was the later fitting of 160 hp Monosoupapes into Camels!'

After the war, the Pup was regarded with affectionate nostalgia by those who had flown it, whether in anger or in training, and it was considered

7

to be a 'nice' aeroplane with which to equip post-war flying clubs. It was not vicious, had few if any vices and tended not to kill or injure pilots if they did something over-stupid.

The RNAS received its first Pup in May 1916 for operational trials with Naval 'A' Squadron – the RNAS did not adopt squadron numbers until later that year. By September early examples of the Sopwith Scout had reached several squadrons, with among the first being 1 Naval Wing. By then the RNAS had progressed from lettered squadrons to numbered wings, and 1 Naval Wing later became 1 Naval Squadron.

FIRST PUP ACES

1 Naval Wing scored the Pup's first victory on 22 September 1916 when Flt Sub-Lt S J Goble (in prototype 3691) sent an LVG two-seater down 'out of control' over Ghistelles, in France, following a raid by several German machines on Dunkirk. Three days later, Flt Sub-Lt E R Grange claimed a German seaplane of *Seeflug 2*, which broke up over the sea following his attack.

Stan Goble had been born in Australia in 1891. He joined the RNAS in 1915, and had already claimed two victories with Nieuport scouts by the time he scored the Pup's first success. Canadian Edward Grange had actually been born in the American state of Michigan in January 1892. Living in Toronto, he had learnt to fly at the Curtiss Flying School in the summer of 1915 and, having joined the RNAS, was sent to 1 Naval Wing early the following year. Both men would become aces on the Sopwith Pup, but not with 1 Naval Wing.

Further south, on the main British Front, the Battle of the Somme had been raging since July, and the RFC was in desperate need of reinforcements. It fell to the RNAS to provide this support through the creation of 8 Naval Squadron, which was formed expressly for service on the Somme battle front under the command of G R Bromet. The new unit was created by taking single flights from each of the Dunkirk Wings, 1 Naval Wing providing six Pups, 4 Naval Wing six Nieuport 11 scouts and 5 Naval Wing six two-seat Sopwith 1½ Strutters.

Two of the pilots moving with the Pups were Goble (having by now been awarded a Distinguished Service Cross (DSC)) and Grange. In fact, virtually every pilot who transferred was a volunteer, as they all saw a move to the Somme front as an opportunity for more action. The new formation transferred south from St Pol to Vert Galand Farm, north of Amiens, on 26 October. After the war, Goble remained in the RAF, and wrote of his experiences while at Staff College. Of the Pup he said;

'In October 1916 my flight was detached complete and formed one of the flights of 8 Naval Squadron. The squadron consisted of one flight of Sopwith 1½ Strutters, one flight of 80 hp Le Rhône Nieuports and the flight of Pups. In December 1916 the other two types were replaced by Pups. All offensive patrols were carried out at high altitudes, with the objective of engaging enemy aircraft between the heights of 10,000 and 20,000 ft. The duration of the patrols was normally three hours, which, in the opinion of all pilots, was too long a period at which to patrol at high altitudes with much diving and climbing, and without oxygen or electrically heated clothing. It appeared to sap our nervous energy, and all pilots felt the strain.'

Goble also recalled the good feeling that existed between the RFC and the RNAS personnel as they worked and fought together.

'Naval 8', as it was often called, replaced the RFC's No 32 Sqn, flying DH 2s, at Vert Galand. Bad weather delayed the departure from St Pol, and then hindered the flight itself once the unit had finally gotten airborne. Only a handful made it to their new home before dark, with the rest dribbling in during the next day or so. Flt Sub-Lt R R Soar was among the 'missing', as he reported;

'Flying Sopwith 1½ Strutter 5102 from Codekerque to the Somme, with Gunlayer George as my observer, we landed at Bruay. No 16 Sqn CO, Maj Maltby, eventually led us over the lines at Lille. We were in the air for one hour and thirty minutes.'

Once at the front, the squadron came under the control of the RFC's 22nd Wing, 5th Brigade, and finally started operating on 3 November. Encounters with enemy aircraft followed one week later, with Flt Sub-Lt Stanley V Trapp forcing a German scout to land on the 10th, while Flt Sub-Lt D M B Galbraith DSC sent another down 'out of control' near Bapaume several hours later.

Murray Galbraith was already a veteran by the time he scored his first Pup victory. Born in Carlton Place, Ontario, in April 1897, he had learned to fly with his friends and future naval aces, Roy Brown and Stearne Edwards. Joining the RNAS, Galbraith had served with 1 Naval Wing and 'A' Squadron, and had claimed three German seaplanes (two while flying a Nieuport and one with a Pup) by the time he got his fourth victory – a Roland scout – on 10 November.

Six days later Goble and Galbraith both downed LVG two-seaters, which brought the latter's score to five. That same day six more Pups arrived from Dunkirk to replace the 'Strutters', making 'Naval 8' a single-seater-only unit. On 17 November Stan Trapp and Stan Goble each claimed another victory, the latter downing a fighter which crashed while its pilot was trying to make a forced landing. It was Goble's fifth victory, while Trapp also saw his two-seater opponent crash. Galbraith took his score to six on the 23rd with an LVG which came down east of Cambrai – one of six he attacked mid-afternoon.

Earlier that day, future ranking 'Naval 8' ace Flt Sub-Lt R A Little had claimed a C-type, which crashed in flames north-east of Bapaume. His combat report stated;

'Saw the hostile aircraft north-east of Bapaume steering south. I also saw two Nieuports, numbers 3956 and 3958, of the RNAS squadron, so I attracted their attention to the hostile machine and then dived at it. It turned east and dived. I began firing from about 150 yards away, and kept up a continuous fire until about 75 yards away, when the hostile machine caught fire, having been hit by tracers. The machine went down at an angle of 85 degrees. Flames and white smoke were coming out of it all the time. I followed it down to about 6500 ft and saw it still burning on the ground close to a small wood.'

Little's victim was probably a machine from FA(A)221, which fell near Etricourt, both crew members being killed. Goble ended the November scoring with another two-seater on the 27th. Like Stan Goble, Bob Little was an Australian, having been born in Melbourne in July 1895. He had joined the RNAS in 1915, and after flying some bombing missions from

Canadian D M B Galbraith DSC and Bar flew Pups with 1 Naval Wing, Naval 'A' Squadron and 'Naval 8'. Four of his six victories were achieved with the Sopwith Scout

Another ace to score early victories with the Pup (three) was Australian R A Little. Bob Little went on to achieve 47 victories before his death in action on 27 May 1918. The leading Australian ace of all time, he was awarded the DSO and Bar and DSC and Bar

Pup N5183 had been flown by Reg Soar while serving with 'Naval 8'. Prior to that it had been allocated to 1 and 2 Naval Wings, where it had been used by future Pup aces Stan Goble and Art Whealy. N5183 is seen here after a less than happy landing 'somewhere in France'

Dunkirk, he transferred to 'Naval 8' to fly Pups. This victory on the 23rd was his first, but it was far from being his last. By May 1918 Little's score had risen to 47 – mostly claimed while flying Sopwith Triplanes – and he had been awarded both the Distinguished Service Order (DSO) and Bar and the DSC and Bar.

A combat-weary Murray Galbraith left the squadron in early December 1916, by which time his actions had won for him a Bar to his DSC. He then spent some considerable time instructing, before being posted to Italy to fly seaplanes. Post-war, Galbraith served in the Royal Canadian Air Force (RCAF) until he was killed in a car accident in 1921.

'Naval 8' had a busy day on 4 December, providing three Pups (which operated alongside four DH 2s from No 32 Sqn) as escorts for the Martinsyde G.100s of No 23 Sqn during a bombing raid on a German aerodrome. After the bombing, the formation patrolled Velu and Ytres and found an unusually large number of German aircraft ranged against them. Both Little and Goble fought like mad during an encounter just prior to noon, and despite the latter being physically sick in the air, he sent a Halberstadt scout down and drove off several others, while Bob Little claimed another destroyed.

Stan Goble returned alone from the engagement, and it was thought that Little had been lost, although he turned up later. The Australian had landed close to the trenches to clear his jammed gun, and had then taken off to continue the action. Later, Little forced down two more Halberstadts. Reggie Soar was in this fight;

'I was flying Pup 3691 on an offensive patrol over Bapaume and Achiet-le-Grand. At Comelles, we dived on an enemy aircraft from 4000 ft. The enemy aircraft was a two-seater Type 6. It was forced to land. I was in the air for two hours and fifteen minutes.'

The day was not over, for Flt Lt C R Mackenzie and Flt Sub-Lt G G Simpson sent another scout down out of control. George Simpson had scored his first and only victory flying a Pup, but he later became an ace on Triplanes. Yet another Australian, he had a total of eight victories by July 1917 and held the DSC. Mackenzie, who was an experienced flight leader, was killed on 24 January 1917. His thoughts on air fighting with the Pup are expressed in some detail in the Appendices.

A week later Goble got his eighth victory when he sent a two-seater down out of control near Bucquoy. His prowess earned him the DSO in the new year, this award being announced in the same batch as the Bar to Galbraith's DSC and DSCs for Grange and Little.

Bad weather curtailed operations until 20 December, when Flt Lt G E Hervey and Flt Sub-Lt A S Todd each claimed a scout, while Flt Sub-Lt R R Soar got two. Reggie Soar had previously flown 'Strutters' with 5 Naval Wing in France, having seen his first action in the Sopwith two-seater with 3 Naval Wing in the Dardanelles. These were to be his only successes with the Pup, but he became an ace while flying Triplanes and ended the war with 12 victories to his name, as well as a DSC. His log-book entry for his Pup claims read as follows;

'Several engagements. I dived on two Halberstadt scouts and got one at close range, the enemy aircraft going down entirely out of control with its engine still on. Later on, picking up the FE 2s, I saw Hervey engaged by a Halberstadt. Hervey dived away. The enemy aircraft did not see me until I was on his tail, and at very close range I gave him a burst, whereupon he went down absolutely out of control (confirmed by Little). My engine then cut out and Little escorted me back. In the air for two hours and thirty minutes.'

On Boxing Day, Flt Cdr B L Huskisson (Bromet's second-in-command, and senior flight commander) sent an Albatros down out of control, Flt Sub-Lt J C Croft shot down a two-seater and Hervey and Flt Sub-Lt N E Woods claimed a Halberstadt. The next day Mackenzie shot down a scout over Achiet-le-Petit, which brought an end to 'Naval 8's' scoring for 1916.

Flt Sub-Lt Grange claimed the unit's first victory of 1917 when he destroyed an Albatros D II and claimed two out of control on the 4th. That same day, Baron Manfred von Richthofen evened the score when he claimed

Although the Pup could usually hold its own against the more powerful German fighting scouts that began to appear over the front in late 1916, examples of the Sopwith Scout were nevertheless lost due to the sheer number of engagements being fought. A626 of 'Naval 8' was one of those aircraft to fall victim to the new German *Jastas*, the Pup being brought down intact by Friedrich Mallinckrodt (seen here posing with his prize) of *Jasta* 6 on 4 January 1917

Charles Booker of 'Naval 8' had achieved 29 victories by the time he was killed in action on 13 August 1918. Only one of his successes came at the controls of a Pup- on 23 January 1917 – although it was his first victory

a victory over the Pup flown by 'Naval 8's' Flt Sub-Lt A S Todd. Although von Richthofen was still new to combat, his assessment of the Pup is interesting. He felt it could hold its own in a dogfight, and its handling and manoeuvrability were good. He thought that he had only managed to down Todd because the British pilot was outnumbered. Flt Sub-Lt Grange was wounded on the 7th, as was Flt Sub-Lt A H S Lawson, although the former also claimed a D II. He wrote in his report;

'I observed a hostile aircraft ahead of me. I attacked him and he got away by means of a steep nose-dive. He appeared to be under control. I then observed one of our Scouts being attacked by two hostile aircraft. I turned round to go to his assistance, but was attacked unawares from behind by a hostile scout. His first burst hit me in the right shoulder and put my arm out of action. Feeling faint owing to the loss of blood, I made for our lines, picked up No 9 Sqn's aerodrome and landed.'

The winter weather hindered flying for most of the next two weeks, but Reggie Soar claimed another victory on the 23rd, as he reported later;

'While flying Pup 5181 on an offensive patrol, the formation split up and fought several individual engagements. I attacked six Halberstadts, sending one down in a spin. Flt Cdr Huskinson later attacked enemy aircraft over Arras. I was in the air for two hours and five minutes.'

In these engagements, Flt Lt C D Booker claimed an Albatros two-seater that he sent down out of control, trailing smoke, north-east of Bapaume. Charles Booker was nearing his 20th birthday, and although Kent-born, he had lived in Australia since 1911. Joining the RNAS in 1915, he was another former 5 Naval Wing pilot who had joined 'Naval 8' in October 1916. This was his first (and only) Pup claim, although he would go on to score a further 28 victories, mostly on Triplanes, win the DSC and *Croix de Guerre* (CdG) and command the RAF's No 201 Sqn. Booker died in combat on 13 August 1918.

Operations continued throughout January and into February, but losses were the main feature. A S Todd had already fallen on the 5th, Mackenzie fell on the 24th and Flt Sub-Lt W E Trayner on 2 February. The latter was a new pilot, as Soar recorded;

'On 1 February I flew Pup 5196 over the Thiepval district, going down to 800 ft to show the lines to Trayner. We attempted a reconnaissance over Achiet-le-Petit, but were driven off by enemy aircraft. In the air for one hour and fifteen minutes. On 2 February I again flew Pup 5196, but this time to Bapaume. Escorting FE 2s taking photographs, I got detached from the aircraft over the lines. I fought my way back to the FE 2s near Cambrai and then had to fight my way back to the aerodrome again. Trayner was killed in combat. We were opposed by scores of enemy fighting scouts. I was in the air for one hour and fifty minutes.'

Trayner had been posted into the unit from 3 Naval Squadron, which was about to move to the Somme. He was brought down by a German two-seater crew of Bavarian FA261, whose pilot, Of Stv Fritz Kosmahl, would become an ace on two-seaters and gain four more victories with *Jasta* 26 before dying of wounds in September 1917.

'NAVAL 8' AND 'NAVAL 3' EXCHANGE

On the same day that W E Trayner was killed, 'Naval 8' was ordered back to Dunkirk following the arrival of 'Naval 3' at Vert Galand. The latter

Pup N5199 served with 'Naval 3' in the early months of 1917, during which time it was flown by future aces E R Grange, L H Rochford and L S Breadner

Fifteen-victory ace J A Glen DSC scored four of his five Pup successes in this machine (N6183), which was named *MILDRED H*, while serving with 'Naval 3' in the spring and summer of 1917

took over 'Naval 8's' Pups too, for the unit was about to receive examples of the new Sopwith Triplane (see *Osprey Aircraft of the Aces 62 – Sopwith Triplane Aces* for further details).

Commanded by R H 'Red' Mulock DSO ('Red' because his first was name Redford, rather than for the colour of his hair), 'Naval 3' received orders for the move south to the Somme at the end of January. The first two flights left by road on 1 February, with the third departing on the 3rd. One of the squadron's pilots was future ace Leonard Rochford, who thought that the Pups they took over at Vert Galand 'were mostly in very poor condition, having completed many flying hours'.

The squadron was not up to total pilot strength either, with Wg Capt C L Lambe, who travelled from Dunkirk to check that the new unit was settling in, stating that several Canadians were about to arrive. 'They are full out for blood', he told the unit. Irishman Flt Sub-Lt Francis Casey retorted that they would get all that 'if they're going to fly these old Pups!' Two days later the new batch of pilots duly arrived – seven Canadians and one Yorkshireman. Among them were several future aces, namely J J Malone, J A Glen, J S T Fall, R Collishaw, F C Armstrong and A T Whealy.

'Naval 3' had by now become a very cosmopolitan unit, boasting Englishmen, Canadians, an Australian, a New Zealander and the Irishman Casey. Having been hard-pressed flying 'Strutters' against the Germans 'up north', the new pilots were looking forward to their single-seaters. They were not impressed to find tired old Pups, however. Ray Collishaw noted in his book *Air Command*;

'The Pups that we received were not all new. Most of them were turned over to us by "Naval 8", which had been flying them since the latter part of 1916, and they had seen much service. Many, in fact, were verging on the worn-out. However, we realised that all we could do was to make the best of what we had, and capitalise on the aircraft's extreme manoeuvrability.'

Len Rochford was just about the youngest and least experienced pilot in 'Naval 3', and during his first take-off in one of the old Pups – 3691 – he learnt a valuable lesson, as he related in his book *I Chose the Sky;*

'When taking off, the tips of the propeller blades struck the ground. As soon as I was airborne there was a

L H 'Titch' Rochford achieved three early successes with the Pup, before going on to score a further 26 victories with 'Naval 3' and No 203 Sqn flying Camels

Despite holding a camera in his hands, it is Canadian ace Jimmy Glen who is the subject of this photograph. Behind his right shoulder, facing the camera, is Fred Armstrong, who, like Glen, scored five victories flying Pups with 'Naval 3' in 1917

violent vibration throughout the machine, and it felt as though it was going to fall to pieces. However, I managed to complete a half circuit of the aerodrome and then land. As far as I can remember, the only damage was to the propeller, and that was beyond repair. This accident impressed on me a particular point about taking-off in a Pup. When flying other aeroplanes I had always got the tail well up off the ground before easing back the joystick to take-off. In the case of the Pup, the propeller had a very small clearance above the ground. Consequently, it was necessary not to get the tail up too high off the ground when taking-off.'

Pup 3691 had to be sent back to Dunkirk for repair, and it was subsequently relegated to Home Defence duties. Later still, this veteran machine was sent to the USA to be displayed in an exhibition. Although it returned to England in 1918 to be preserved as a museum exhibit, the Sopwith fighter was, like so many other machines from World War 1, finally scrapped.

The squadron had its first encounter with German aircraft on 14 February, when Flt Lt R G Mack drove down a two-seater near Warlencourt. At noon the next day, Raymond Collishaw, destined to be third-ranking British and Commonwealth air ace of World War 1, sent down a Halberstadt scout out of control over Bapaume. It was his third victory, the first two having been claimed while flying $1^1/2$ Strutters with 1 Naval Wing the previous October. Collishaw wrote the following account of his first combat experiences with the Pup;

'My first combat with "Naval 3" came on 14 February. I had been assigned to "C" Flight, and we took off for a line patrol at 14,000 ft between Warlencourt and Rossignal. I was flying Sopwith Pup N6160. We were at our specified height over Vaux when my flight commander, accompanied by one of the other pilots, turned to attack a German two-seater that came into sight. As they did so, I saw another two-seater below me and dived down, getting behind him. I was in a good position when I opened fire, but my Vickers jammed and I had to turn away while I struggled to clear the gun.

'I had just cleared the stoppage when I saw a German single-seater approaching, evidently with the idea of lending a hand to the two-seaters. I turned towards him and opened fire, but again my gun jammed. Try as I could, I was not able to clear the obstruction. With a useless gun there was nothing to do but to turn back to Vert Galand.

'A combat the following day ended more satisfactorily. Again on a line patrol, I attacked a two-seater. I was not able to accomplish much against its pilot and observer, but some minutes afterwards we spotted two scouts flying towards our lines and I attacked one of them. I fired several bursts, 40 rounds in all, from about 200 ft and the German went down in a spin. I followed him down, but my engine had been hit during the combat and it faltered and then cut out completely. I was fortunate to make it back into our own territory, landing safely just north of Albert. The RFC communiqué reported that I had sent the enemy scouts down out of control, although in my youthful vanity I was a little piqued to read that credit for the affair was given to one Flt Sub-Lt Collinson.'

On 1 March, Flt Sub-Lt H E P Wrigglesworth sent another scout down smoking, but the day was marred for another new Pup squadron whose first combat took place back on the Channel coast.

When 'Naval 8' returned to Dunkirk, a nucleus of its pilots went to 9 Naval Squadron, formed at St Pol on 1 February 1917. What few Pups and Nieuport 17s were left went to the new unit, which would also be receiving Triplanes. Its first action, though, came on 1 March while it still had the Pup. Flt Sub-Lt F V Branford engaged two German seaplanes along the coast and, it is understood, shot one down. But his Pup (N6164) was damaged by return fire, forcing him to ditch near the Zeeland town of Cadzanal. He was rescued by the Dutch, but was interned. The Pup too was salvaged, repaired and eventually used by its new owners.

FIRST RFC PUP UNIT

By late 1916 the RFC had realised the Sopwith Pup's virtues and purchased a number for frontline service. The writing was on the wall for 'pusher' scouts like the DH 2 and FE 8 now that the new German fighters were coming into service with the recently formed *Jastas*. The Pup was one of the first Sopwith designs bought by the RFC, and No 54 Sqn ushered the type into service in October 1916 while engaged on Home Defence duties from Castle Bromwich.

The squadron was sent to France on 24 December, and on 11 January it commenced operations from Chipilly. No 54 Sqn was commanded by Maj K K Horn MC, and following a period of adjustment, Capt Alan Lees achieved the unit's first success on the morning of 25 January. This action, fought at 1030 hrs, involved a German scout. The unit combat report stated;

'While on patrol at about 16,000 ft, Capt Lees saw Lt Hamilton attack a hostile aircraft below him. He dived down on the hostile aircraft as well and drove him down to 4000 ft (using about 120 rounds) when his gun jammed badly. He made for the lines and, on looking round, saw the hostile aircraft stall and do a vertical dive with its left top plane badly damaged (i.e. part of it trailing behind). Capt Lees lost sight of the hostile

Pup A635 of No 66 Sqn is seen shortly after it was shot down by Theodor Quandt of *Jasta* 36 on 12 October 1917. Nine months earlier, on 25 January, Capt Alan Lees had claimed No 54 Sqn's first victories in this Pup on 25 January 1917. His two claims on this day also represented the first successes for the RFC with the Pup

What was William H Chisam thinking when he posed in front of N6162 *"I WONDER"* ? – note his very non-regulation footwear. He failed to score any victories in the Pup, but went on to down seven aircraft while flying Camels with 'Naval 3'. This particular aircraft was also flown by L H Rochford and H S Broad, both of whom scored victories with it

aircraft before it reached the ground, but it was coming down in the vicinity of Morancourt Wood, north of Péronne.'

Twenty minutes, later in a second encounter;

'A hostile aircraft approached four de Havillands and Capt Lees and did a steep downwards spiral. Capt Lees followed from 8000 ft to 3000 ft, firing about 120 rounds when his gun jammed. Two de Havillands and Capt Lees followed the hostile aircraft down to the ground, where it was surrounded by soldiers.'

A pencil notation on the first report indicated that this claim was to be counted as crashed, while the second noted merely as 'yes', for the two-seater had come down on the Allied side of the lines near Maricourt.

Two days later, 2Lt F N Hudson MC claimed a third victory for No 54 Sqn when he downed a two-seater near Courcelette at 1410 hrs.

Frank Neville Hudson from Beckenham, Kent, was 19 years old, and he had transferred to the RFC from the East Kent Regiment. Having seen much action flying BE 2s with No 15 Sqn in 1916 prior to requesting a move to single-seaters, he would eventually become an ace on Pups. Hudson's second victory, over another two-seater, crashed near Le Transloy on 13 February.

'Naval 3' found itself in the thick of the action during the late morning of 4 March, the unit having moved to Bertangles from Vert Galand on 28 February. Its pilots became embroiled with a mixed formation of Albatros and Halberstadt scouts, four of which it claimed as shot down out of control during the final hour of the morning – one each by Collishaw, 'Titch' Rochford, T C Vernon and J J Malone.

It was a bright but cold morning, and everyone had expected to meet the enemy. Some of the squadron escorted FE 2s on an operation, while R G Mack and Rochford were to escort Moranes. The latter two pilots were attacked by five Albatros scouts as they headed back towards Allied lines. Rochford recorded;

'Over Manancourt we were attacked by five Albatros scouts, and for the first time I was in a scrap with German fighters. I heard the "rat-tat-tat" of their Spandau guns and felt frightened as I manoeuvred my Pup to prevent one getting his sights on me. Suddenly, a mottled brown and black Albatros dived from the right, in front of me, to attack Mack.

Two stalwarts of 'Naval 3' in the early spring of 1917 were A W 'Nick' Carter DSC and J J 'Jack' Malone DSO

Canadian Pup ace 'Jack' Malone had claimed ten victories with the Sopwith Scout by the time he was killed in action on 30 April 1917 by Paul Billik of *Jasta* 12

Quickly, I fired a burst at him. He fell away sideways and I lost sight of him as I looked for the other enemy aircraft. They had broken off the fight and were diving steeply away eastwards.'

Mack confirmed seeing the scout completely out of control. Such victories were always difficult to confirm, for pilots of both sides often spun away from trouble, but the British airmen, fighting mostly over German territory, and being unable to confirm that their victims had actually crashed, claimed what were in essence 'probables', although many times they were not even 'possibles'!

John Joseph 'Jack' Malone was a Canadian, although born in the USA in December 1894. Initially serving with 3 Naval Wing flying 'Strutters', he had joined 3 Naval Squadron as it was forming. The action on 4 March brought him his first success, and in the next few weeks he would become an ace and win the DSO.

'Titch' Rochford was also destined to become an ace, and he too had opened his account on this day. He would eventually gain 29 victories before war's end, the first three of them on Pups. Rochford also received the DSC and Bar and the DFC, and would survive more than 70 air battles. The Author, who met him many years ago, considers Rochford to have been a great little man, and one of the world's gentlemen.

The other Naval Pup pilots who had sortied on 4 March also encountered enemy opposition, and while they had claimed three aircraft destroyed, two Pups were downed in return – both credited to pilots of *Jasta* 1. Another loss this same day was Capt Lees of No 54 Sqn, who became a prisoner of war (PoW) after being brought down wounded by Lt Georg Schlenker of *Jasta* 3. Schlenker would later become a 14-victory ace with *Jastas* 3 and 41. This was his second No 54 Sqn Pup victory, taking his score to four.

'Naval 3' claimed two more out-of-control victories in the Vaux area shortly before noon on the 11th – a two-seater by H G Travers and an Albatros D III by Flt Cdr B C Bell.

Herbert Gardner Travers – known as 'Tiny' – was born on 1 April 1891, so his 27th birthday would fall on the day the RAF was established. He had transferred to the RNAS from the Honourable Artillery Company, where he had

Flt Cdr H G Travers initially served with 1 Naval Wing before joining 'Naval 3', with whom he gained five victories flying Pups in March and April 1917. He was awarded the DSC for his success with the scout

Irishman Francis D Casey DSC claimed nine Pup victories between 17 March and 2 May 1917 whilst serving with 'Naval 3'

been a machine gunner. Joining 1 Naval Wing in May 1916, he had flown scouts during that year, before being posted to 'Naval 3'. Travers would win the DSC and claim five victories in March and April 1917.

Returning to 11 March, at 1230 hrs Capt R Oxspring of No 54 Sqn destroyed another two-seater near Bapaume. The unit's pilots were escorting No 22 Sqn FE 2s on a reconnaissance mission at the time when a German C-type had had the audacity to attack one of the big pushers. Oxspring quickly got on the tail of the German aircraft, which dived steeply, followed by the Pup pilot. The latter eventually had to pull out as the enemy's dive became too great to follow. Crews of No 22 Sqn watched as the C-type hit the ground shortly after losing a wing.

At around this time No 54 Sqn became well known for its song book, the words written mostly by F J 'Inf' Morse. One of his tune's went as follows;

Oh! We came out from Birmingham
To see the great big war –
There was Oxo right chock full of fight,
And Nobby out for gore.
Archie shot at us 'Gr-r-umph! Umph!'
And blacked the sky so blue,
When right up flew a Halberstadt
And said, 'And vitch vos you?'
Chorus: *Oh we've come up from Fifty Four;*
We're the Sopwith Pups, you know.
And wherever you dirty swine may be
The Sopwith Pups will go.
And if you want a proper scrap,
Don't chase 2Cs anymore;
For we'll come up and do the job,
Because we're FIFTY FOUR.

In some early lists of aces, No 54 Sqn's Robert Oxspring has been incorrectly credited with 16 victories. Formally with the King's Own Yorkshire Light Infantry, he transferred to the RFC and flew with No 12 Sqn, before becoming a fighter pilot. He then served with both Nos 54 and 66 Sqns on Pups, gaining a few victories. To the MC, gained while serving with the Light Infantry, he was able to add a Bar during his time with the RFC, and he ended the war as a major. Oxspring's son, also Robert (Bobby), became a noted Spitfire ace (with 13.5 victories to his credit) in World War 2, winning the DFC and Bar.

'Naval 3's' Jack Malone had a field day on 17 March, when he scored two victories in the morning and a third in the afternoon. The naval boys got stuck into some scouts and a two-seater near Bapaume, Malone sending the latter down in a spin. In the subsequent scrap with several Halberstadt and Albatros scouts, he sent one of the latter down in flames. Bell followed suit with a Halberstadt, as did F D Casey for his first victory, while Travers claimed another Albatros for his second victory.

Francis Dominic Casey was born in August 1890 in Clonmee, Ireland. He joined the RNAS in May 1916, and had flown as an observer with 2 Naval Wing. Following pilot training, Casey joined 'Naval 3', and he

Flt Cdr Casey DSC poses in front of one of the first Camels to reach 'Naval 3' at Furnes in July 1917. Returning from leave, he took one of the new fighters up and was duly killed in a crash while 'stunting' over the airfield on 11 August

would eventually claim nine victories with this unit. Winning the DSC, Casey was subsequently killed when he crashed a newly delivered Sopwith Camel B3805 in August 1917.

The morning of 17 March also brought success to No 54 Sqn, when a four-aircraft patrol intercepted a two-seater east of Roye and sent it down out of control. The patrol was comprised of Capt R G H Pixley and Lts N A Phillips, G A Hyde MC and J W Sheridan.

George Arthur Hyde had won his MC with the King's Royal Rifle Corps in 1916 prior to joining the RFC. A Yorkshireman from Easingwold, he was born in July 1893 and had attended Peterhouse, Cambridge. He too would become an ace. In an article written long after the war, Hyde recalled;

'Work in the air was pretty active. The Germans were beginning to fly around in formations of increased numbers, and it became the usual thing to have a scrap with the enemy on each offensive patrol. I well remember my first real fight. It was just after we moved, and a patrol of us, led by Capt Strugnell, was escorting Martinsydes to Busigny at 14,000 ft. A dozen or more Albatros D IIIs dived on us, and the first realisation I had that anything was wrong was when a dreadful cracking sounded in my ears – a Hun was on my tail. We all got home safely. Strugnell, who brought down one of the enemy, arrived back with his tailplane shot to ribbons, and most of us had several holes in our machines, but the scrap

'Naval 3' aces E Pierce, E T Hayne, A T Whealy and H F Beamish were photographed in front of their billets at Liettres in early April 1917. They do not seem to be overly bothered by the cameraman's presence

gave me confidence in the Pup as a fighting instrument, for I found that it could out-manoeuvre an Albatros in turns.'

And it was No 54 Sqn that scored next. On 19 March, Capt W V Strugnell and Lt E J Y Grevelink (the squadron artist) claimed a two-seater in flames – one of two the patrol had engaged over Roisel at 0745 hrs. Strugnell had a duel with the observer before his gun jammed and he broke away, but Grevelink saw the observer stop firing as if hit. He then followed up the attack, and the two-seater burst into flames and went down. It may have been a machine from FA 8.

William Victor Strugnell came from a regular Army family, having been born in July 1892 near Southampton. At 15 he joined the Royal Engineers – his father was a mechanical sergeant major – as a bugler, and was later a sapper with the Hampshire Regiment. Volunteering as an air mechanic, Strugnell learned to fly in 1912, being only the third non-commissioned airman to receive a flying certificate. Serving with Nos 3 and 5 Sqns pre-war, he went to France with No 1 Sqn during 1915–16, claiming at least one victory while flying a Morane. Commissioned, and now with the MC, Strugnell later moved to No 54 Sqn as a flight commander. He would score five more victories in Pups, and gain a Bar to his MC in July 1917.

The RNAS were in action again on 24 March when 'Naval 3's' Flt Cdr Bell shot down a Halberstadt, and 'Naval 9's' Flt Sub-Lt H S Kerby destroyed a seaplane near Wenduyne at about 1100 hrs for his first victory. Canadian Harold Spencer Kerby was born in Alberta, Calgary, in May 1893. An engineer, he joined the RNAS in 1915 and first saw action in the Dardanelles with 3 Naval Wing. Once back in England, he joined 'Naval 9', and having claimed this solitary victory on 24 March, was posted to 'Naval 3', with whom he would become an ace.

The spring weather brought with it an increase in air activity over the Western Front. Both Allied and German leaders were planning spring offensives, but it was the Allied side that struck first. On the Arras front, the high ground of Vimy Ridge was an essential target in a landscape that was predominantly flat. The battle to take the ridge would see much carnage on the ground. In the air, the RFC and the RNAS would clash in earnest with the new German *Jastas* during a period that would see Allied airmen suffer their worst casualties of the entire war. History would name this month 'Bloody April'.

'BLOODY APRIL'

The British offensive at Arras was planned to open on Easter Monday, 9 April 1917, and the Allies tried hard to conceal their preparations for the campaign. The scout squadrons helped to ensure that German airmen did not see too many signs of troop movement, increased road and rail traffic and ammunition dumps being established.

As part of this operation, No 54 Sqn chased off two two-seaters on the 2nd. Capt Oxspring damaged one and Lt O M Sutton sent the second machine down near Péronne, its observer hit and disappearing into his rear cockpit prior to the aircraft crashing.

Oliver Manners Sutton had gained his first victory on his way to becoming an ace. Born in Tunbridge Wells, Kent, in March 1896, the former engineering student had served with the South Lancashire Regiment prior to becoming a pilot. Having flown two-seaters with No 21 Sqn, Sutton transferred to fighters and joined No 54 Sqn in late 1916.

There was also a need to keep German kite balloons from observing too much, and No 54 Sqn was given the task of dealing with them too. On the 5th, Oxspring, together with Capt Hudson and Lts M D G Scott, R G H Pixley and R M Charley, attacked and destroyed a balloon east of Vendeville. On the way back, some of the pilots shot up targets on the ground, including troops standing by lorries at a railway station and a soldier on horseback.

Leading Pup ace J S T Fall DSC of 'Naval 3' poses in front of Lloyd Breadner's Pup N6181 *HMA HAPPY*. Joe Fall scored no fewer than 11 victories with the Pup. Note that N6181's cowling has been painted in its flight colour (red)

N6178 *BABY MINE* was flown by 'Nick' Carter of 'Naval 3', who claimed three of his five Pup victories while flying it on 23 and 29 April 1917. The aircraft later served with the Seaplane Defence Flight at Dunkirk, where it was used by seven-victory ace L H Slatter to badly damage a Gotha bomber at night in September 1917

Both Maurice Scott and Reg Charley would later become aces. Maurice Douglas Guest Scott came from Felixstowe, although he was born in Dorset in 1895 (various records state August, September or November), and he had seen service with the Loyal North Lancs. Upon joining the RFC, he had initially served as an observer with No 18 Sqn, flying Vickers FB 5s. During this period, Scott and his pilot had brought down a two-seater inside Allied lines. Subsequently learning to fly, he would go on to add 11 more scalps to his tally during his tour with Nos 54 and 46 Sqns. Scott would also win the MC.

Although Reginald Morse Charley – born in 1892 – participated in this balloon attack, he does not appear to have shared in the spoils. Nevertheless, he had become an ace by the late summer, and would receive the MC and French CdG. Charley had been in America just prior to the war, and once hostilities had commenced he had travelled to Canada and joined the RFC, learning to fly in Toronto.

On the 6 April both 'Naval 3' and No 54 Sqn were in action. Shortly after dawn, the latter unit's Hudson and Stewart downed a two-seater and a scout respectively, and several hours later the squadron claimed no fewer than five Halberstadt scouts while escorting bombers. Those involved were T C Vernon, J S T Fall, F C Armstrong, A W Carter and L S Breadner. The latter four – all Canadians – were all starting their scoring runs that would see them achieve ace status with the Pup.

Joseph Stewart Temple Fall was born in November 1895 on a farm at Hillbank, on Vancouver Island in British Columbia. Becoming an RNAS pilot after travelling to England in January 1916, he was sent to France and had been with 'Naval 3' for some time. But only now did Fall begin to rain destruction upon the enemy with this, his first of 36 victories (11 of which would be achieved while flying Pups). He would go on to win no fewer than three DSCs and an Air Force Cross – the only Canadian to do so.

In his report for the 6th, Fall wrote;

'Our formation was attacked by four hostile aircraft. One dived at me from in front and carried on diving. I did a half loop and dived too, following him down to 4000 ft. I fired about 50 rounds at him, saw many tracers enter his fuselage and he went down out of control. From about 1000 ft he spun to the ground, and I saw him crash. I saw two other hostile machines, one of which was going down apparently out of control, stalling and diving and then went into a spin.'

Fall was far from being the only Canadian RNAS Pup ace. Frederick Carr 'Army' Armstrong, who would gain 13 victories (five on Pups), was born in Toronto in June 1895 and had already seen action with 3 Naval Wing.

Alfred William 'Nick' Carter, born in Fish Creek, Calgary, in April 1894, also arrived at 'Naval 3' via 3 Naval Wing. Five of his eventual

17 claims would be made with the Pup, the others being achieved on Camels with 10 Naval Squadron.

Finally, Lloyd Samuel 'Bread' Breadner, born in July 1894 in Carlton Place, Ontario, was yet another 3 Naval Wing veteran. Seven of his ten claims would come with the Pup.

NO 66 SQN JOINS THE FRAY

The second RFC Pup squadron to be sent into action arrived in France in early March 1917. No 66 Sqn, which had formed at Filton in June 1916 but had since been employed as a training unit, flew to St Omer, then to Vert Galand, under the command of Maj O T Boyd MC. It began operations just in time for the Arras offensive, and had its first encounters the day before the battle started. An afternoon patrol, led by Capt G W Roberts, got into a scrap with some Halberstadt scouts and four were reported to have gone down out of control.

Not far away, 'Naval 3' was in a fight with a formation of Albatros D IIIs, during which 'Tiny' Travers and Francis Casey each claimed one out of control north-east of Pronville.

Canadian 'Nick' Carter DSC eventually claimed 17 victories, and ended the war as CO of Camel-equipped No 210 Sqn. Aside from his five Pup victories, he subsequently claimed four destroyed with Triplanes and eight with Camels

'Naval 3's' Lloyd Breadner DSC is seen at Marieux with his *HMA HAPPY*. Five of his seven Pup victories were claimed in this machine between 11 and 29 April 1917

At dawn on the 9th the Battle of Arras commenced. It opened with the usual artillery barrage, but fog curtailed many of the intended air operations – the battle area was also blanketed by smoke from exploding shells. This continued the next day, with strong wind and snow making things worse. However, on the 11th 'Naval 3's' Pups met German fighters near Cambrai just before 0900 hrs. Three aircraft were claimed destroyed, with two more out of control. An Albatros two-seater was also downed. Two scouts, with a third sent down smoking, were accounted for by Joe Fall, while Lloyd Breadner got another scout and the C-type. The latter wrote in his combat report;

'Escort to bombers, Cambrai 0900 hrs, in Pup N6181. While between Marquion and Cambrai, I was attacked from above and behind by an Albatros (two-seater). I turned left, and while broadside on, the observer opened fire. I again turned left and the Albatros immediately manoeuvred to come down on my tail again. We were both firing. I pulled my machine up into a stall as he was about to pass over me (about 20 yards above me) and riddled him with bullets. When I turned on him again, he was going down in a spin, and flames were shooting out of the fuselage. I therefore claim one two-seat Albatros, mottled green and yellow (swept back wings), destroyed.'

Pup N5185 was lost, however, when future 'Naval 3'/No 203 Sqn Camel ace South African E T 'Bollocky' Hayne became the eighth victim of Adolf Schulte of *Jasta* 12. Although his Pup was wrecked, Hayne crashed on the right side of the trenches and escaped with little more than severe shock. He did not score until August 1917, but had achieved 15 victories by the Armistice, and was awarded the DSC and DFC. Hayne died in a flying accident in April 1919.

The RNAS Pup pilots saw more action on the morning of 12 April near Pronville, when another four scouts were claimed driven out of control. Again, it was the up-and-coming aces who scored, Flt Sub-Lts E Pierce and F C Armstrong getting one apiece and sharing another, with A T Whealy claiming the fourth.

Edmund Pierce of 'Naval 3' scored five victories between 12 April and 2 May while flying N6171 'P'. The aircraft fell victim to strong winds at Marieux on 14 April, but it received only superficial damage. Note the name *BLACK ARROW*, and arrow motif painted beneath it

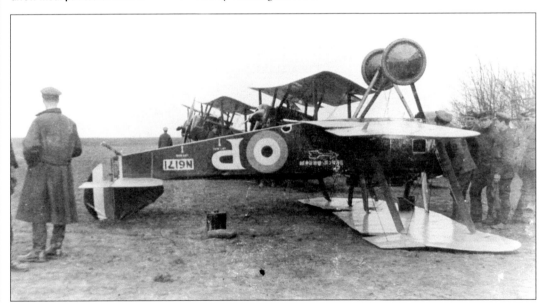

Edmond Pierce, born in October 1896 (although it appears he gave his birth year as 1893), was aged 20. He had opened his account in style, and would gain five victories with the Pup, then another with 'Naval 9'. He scored a seventh with a Triplane, before returning to No 203 Sqn in 1918 to add two more with a Camel. By the time he returned to England in May 1918, Pierce he had flown no fewer than 375 missions during 16 months of war, yet he had only received a Mention in Despatches in July 1917.

Pup N6172 of 'Naval 3' was named *BLACK TULIP* and flown by Flt Lt R G Mack. It is seen here bearing German markings after its capture on 12 April 1917, when it was forced down by Paul von Osterroht of *Jasta* 12. It represented his fifth victory of seven

Arthur Treloar 'Art' Whealy, who was born in Toronto in November 1893, had joined the RNAS in Canada. Yet another pilot to reach the frontline via 3 Naval Wing, he too would become an ace on Pups with 3 and 9 Naval Squadrons, before returning to No 203 Sqn on Camels, where he would take his score to 27 by early September 1918. Whealy won the DSC and Bar, plus the DFC.

Flt Lt R G Mack did not survive this action, however, as he fell wounded after an attack by Paul von Osterroht of *Jasta* 12 to become a PoW. It was the German's fifth victory, but before the month was out, Osterroht would himself fall to 'Naval 3'. Robin Mack's Pup (N6172) was captured intact and was well photographed. It had the letter 'M' on the fuselage sides aft of the cockade, and written beneath the cockpit was the name *BLACK TULIP*. This should not be confused with the names given to the Triplanes of Ray Collishaw's 'Black' Flight in 'Naval 10' later in the year, although the naming obviously stemmed from this period. 'Titch Rochford' wrote;

'Mack's Pup was named *BLACK TULIP*, and of the other machines in "C" Flight, mine was *BLACK BESS*, Collishaw's *BLACK MARIA* and Whealy's *BLACK PRINCE*. All "C" Flight's engine cowlings were painted black, "B" Flight's red and "A" Flight's blue.'

Oxspring, now flying with No 66 Sqn, claimed a two-seater on the 13th over Douai, while Capt Strugnell and 2Lt M W B Cole from his former unit, No 54 Sqn, claimed two more the next day. The latter engaged two C-types shortly after 0800 hrs, and Strugnell saw both quickly turn east and start to dive away. Firing at them from long range, he watched as the two-seater began to dive even more steeply, but Strugnell then suffered a gun jam and had to break off. Another pilot saw the two-seater heading earthwards in a vertical nose dive.

This particular engagement was Mortimer Cole's first exposure to combat. Born in July 1896, he had joined No 54 Sqn in mid-March. The combat report states that '2Lt Cole dived and engaged the hostile aircraft over Gonnelieu and drove him from 10,000 ft down to 6000 ft, where he was left, apparently going down out of control. 2Lt Cole had closed right in just before leaving the hostile aircraft, as the observer had stopped firing and was hanging over the side.'

Despite further intense air operations, the next successful Pup actions did not occur until 21 April, and it was the naval pilots who were engaged. During a late afternoon patrol, 'Naval 3' met two-seaters and Albatros scouts. Flt Lt H G Travers was leading, and he dived on the enemy machines over Cagnicourt. At 1730 hrs he sent one down in a spin, as did F D Casey over Hendicourt, and minutes later he and H S Broad attacked another, which they saw crash. J J Malone went after a two-seater and sent it down out of control north of Queant for his fifth victory. His first four had been scored while flying Pup 9898, but this was his first in N6208 – the machine in which he would score victories five to nine.

The next morning No 66 Sqn encountered Halberstadt scouts near Vitry, Capt J O Andrews claiming one driven down, while 2Lt J T Collier shot down another which was seen to crash. Andrews then engaged an Albatros two-seater, which he also drove down. That evening, Pierce of 'Naval 3' claimed an Albatros scout out of control near Cambrai, and Flt Sub-Lt H S Kerby did the same with an Albatros two-seater. Kerby, it will be remembered, had scored his first victory with 'Naval 9', but had now moved to 'Naval 3'.

Lancastrian John Oliver Andrews was born in July 1896. After serving with the Royal Scottish Regiment he transferred to the RFC, initially as an observer with No 5 Sqn. He then learned to fly, and served with DH 2-equipped No 24 Sqn under the command of Lanoe Hawker VC, DSO. Andrews won the MC and Bar and gained seven victories with this unit. After a brief rest, he became a flight commander with No 66 Sqn.

'DRIVEN DOWN'

The two combats on the 22nd did not result in confirmed victories for either the RFC or RNAS, however. Some of the aircraft 'driven down' in 1915-16 had been noted in a pilot's score, but the terminology was often obscure. 'Driven down', 'driven down – forced to land' and 'driven down – out of control' were sometimes mixed up, leaving the poor historian to try and figure out the exact nature of the claim. By 1917 it was usually clear. 'Driven down' meant just that, while 'driven away' or 'driven off' meant, in reality – and to the pilots at the time – not necessarily put out of action, but just sent packing!

If driving off or driving down a two-seater does not seem so glamorous as one that was actually seen to crash, it should be remembered that at the time, the attacking pilot had succeeded in forcing the two-seater crew to end their mission. This could have been a bombing raid, a photographic sortie, artillery directing or just reconnaissance. Whatever its nature, it had been curtailed, and that still represented a valuable achievement.

It took some time for a two-seater to climb to its operating height. If driven down and away from its area of operations, the pilot might well decide it would take too long – and use too much petrol – to try to regain the lost height, and therefore he would decide to go home. Thus, the attacking single-seater had cut short the two-seater's work, and probably saved lives on the ground from bombs or artillery. Driving down a single-seater also curbed the pilot's activities, and might well have saved some brother pilot or a friendly two-seater crew from being attacked.

John Andrews' attacks on 22 April had been a success, but had not been deemed a 'victory', even though the pilot or observer of the opposing

Capt J O Andrews DSO MC was a highly experienced fighter pilot by the time he joined No 66 Sqn as a flight commander in early April 1917, having already claimed seven victories flying DH 2s with No 24 Sqn. He went on to add five more successes to his tally with the Pup between 30 April and 11 July 1917

aircraft might have been killed or wounded, although the final plunge had not been seen by anyone on the opposition's side. Not everything in war is black and white.

Adding the number of claims to losses soon makes it apparent that both warring sides were not destroying anything like as many enemy aircraft as they thought. With most of the air actions taking place over German-held territory, the *Jasta* pilots had a far better chance of having claims confirmed, as there were wrecks and bodies to provide proof. The RFC and RNAS fighter pilots could only hope that the enemy aeroplane that went spinning down into cloud eventually crashed, unseen by them. The fact that pilots of both sides readily put their aircraft into a spin if they found themselves in a tight spot often seems to have been overlooked.

This was all too apparent on 24 April 1917, when the Pup pilots alone claimed more than 20 German aircraft shot down, but their opposition did not lose anything like that number. There were losses, but most combats resulted in possible damage to an aircraft or perhaps a slight wound to the pilot, but nothing sufficient to put either out of action for very long.

As far as the Pups units were concerned, actions came in the early morning or late afternoon throughout April. For example, on the 23rd Jack Malone claimed an Albatros scout destroyed at 0630 hrs hours near Croiselles, and 45 minutes later he sent another down out-of-control and drove down a third probably also out of control. Early in the same battle, Travers, Pierce, Beamish and G B Anderson also claimed out of control victories, yet no German *Jasta* lost seven fighters that morning. At 0800 hrs, J O Andrews of No 66 Sqn drove down an Albatros two-seater, but again this was not considered a creditable victory.

The exception to the early morning/late afternoon rule came at 1030 hrs on the 23rd, when 'Naval 3' pilot Flt Lt Lloyd Breadner

Another mishap. 'Naval 3's' G B Anderson tipped N6195 'G' onto its nose at St Pol in May 1917. The aircraft's undercarriage appears to have collapsed, which may indicate a heavy landing

encountered the enemy. Despite scoring just three victories to date, Breadner was an experienced aviator, and he was already known to be a bit of a 'fire eater'. The Germans rarely flew their large bombers over the front in daylight, but they did on 23 April, just as Breadner was preparing to go to the hangars at Marieux to retrieve his Pup for a patrol. As he wrote in a letter home;

'I was going down to the aerodrome when I heard anti-aircraft guns going. On looking up, I saw a Hun directly overhead at about 10,000 ft. So I scrambled into my "bus" and went after him. He was at 12,000 ft when I got up to him (a great big double-engined pusher type machine), so I sat right behind his tail where he couldn't shoot at me. I fired 190 rounds and shot both his engines.'

The German machine crashed inside Allied lines near Vron, which enabled Breadner to hastily land in a nearby field and survey his victim at close quarters. The crew had been taken prisoner by this time, and he was unable to talk to them because he did not speak German and they knew no English. Although the Gotha G II was burning, Breadner was able to cut one of the iron crosses from it before the bomber was totally destroyed by fire. He later nailed the trophy to the wall of the squadron mess.

Breadner's Gotha was the first of its type to be brought down over the Western Front by a fighter pilot. It came from *Kampfstaffel* 15 of KG III, and its crew of OfStv (Warrant Officer pilot) Alfred Heidner, Ltn Kurt Karl von Scheuren (observer) and Ltn Otto Wirth were all driven away to captivity. The two officers ended up in Donnington prison camp, in England, while the NCO languished in Frongoch. The Gotha's number was 610/16, but the wreckage acquired the new RFC identity of G23 in the series given to captured aeroplanes and wrecks.

On the afternoon of the 23rd, pilots from 'Naval 3', including Breadner, were escorting six No 18 Sqn RFC FE 2bs on a raid on Epinoy aerodrome when they were engaged by German fighters and had to fight their way back to their lines. Art Whealy and Nick Carter each claimed victories while protecting the FE 2bs until they were safely back over Allied territory. Once free of their charges, the Pup pilots turned to engage the Albatros scouts, and Breadner shot one down trailing smoke over Bourlon Wood. Joe Fall claimed another out of control, while Armstrong, Carter and Casey also put in claims.

A short while later, during a fight over Le Pave, H S Kerby saw two Halberstadts (or perhaps still more Albatros scouts) collide and fall during his attack. He was credited with the destruction of both. Kerby wrote in his report;

'After an indecisive fight with an Albatros, I saw two Halberstadt scouts flying side by side and climbing, about 2000 ft below. I approached down-sun, but evidently was observed by the pilot of one of the machines, who appeared to attempt to warn the other by crossing over him. While doing this, the two hostile aircraft collided, the undercarriage of the upper crashing into the upper plane of the lower. Both machines went down, crashing through the sky.'

A little earlier, at 1630 hrs, J O Andrews of No 66 Sqn had driven down another Albatros two-seater near Vitry, but again it would not be added to his overall score. Andrews, who remained in the RAF post-war, wrote of his Pup experiences while at Staff College. He noted;

'The poor speed and climb and inadequate armament of the Pup developed the formation flying of the flight to the extent that it was able to withstand attacks by superior numbers of aircraft of better performance, without being scattered. The good manoeuvrability of the Pup at altitude, due to its low wing loading, was a great asset. The importance of good formation flying and of mutual confidence and knowledge was emphasised by the experience of one flight, which, owing to early casualties first to its flight commander and then to its flying officers, was never able to settle down, and had more casualties than the other two flights combined.

'If it was difficult to bring down aircraft in 1916 with a Lewis gun firing unrestrictedly in a DH 2, it was desolating to attempt it in a Pup in 1917 with one Vickers gun fitted with a Kauper gear. Enemy aircraft were frequently stalked to within close range, only to escape because the volume of one's fire was inadequate.

'The pattern of a machine gun fired from a vibrating, fast-moving aeroplane is large, and to adequately fill the pattern requires a number of guns. If the "period of surprise" during which an enemy aircraft will afford a steady target is taken as five seconds, and the pattern at 100 yards range as 20 ft square – i.e. 400 square ft – then to average one bullet for each square foot of that space in the five seconds available needs a rate of fire of nearly 5000 rounds a minute!

'In May 1917 I abandoned the tracer bullet, as the general opinion was that it was most misleading, its only value being that of an incendiary bullet. I substituted an armour-piercing bullet, of which two boxes were procured by the good offices of the wing commander.'

The Kauper gear referred to by Andrews was an interrupter system developed in 1916 by H A Kauper, working with the Sopwith Company. By the end of 1917 it had been replaced in RFC fighters mainly by Constantinesco-Colley equipment.

This action made it 17 claims for 'Naval 3' on the 23rd. Added to these were two more Albatros scouts driven down by F W Williams and Collier of No 66 Sqn at 1910 hrs above Lechuse. The latter would be wounded on 4 May.

No 66 Sqn's Capt J O Andrews sits in his Pup B1703, displaying the number 1 on its engine cowling, at Vert Galand in April 1917. He claimed the last three of his five Pup victories with this machine on 13 May, 7 June and 11 July 1917

A M Shook's Pup *BOBS* (N6200) of 'Naval 4' was well photographed. Here, Shook (left) is pictured with his groundcrew

Another shot of *BOBS*, with Shook (left) and other 'Naval 4' pilots at Bray Dunes in May 1917. The pilot on the far right is G W Hemming DSC, who claimed six victories, three of which were on Pups

The only known casualty of note on the German side was the leader of *Jasta* 12, Hptm Paul Henning Aldabert Theodor von Osterroht, who was killed at 1800 hrs near Cambrai in action with 'Naval 3'.

Jasta 33 was also involved in this action, and it had one pilot wounded, although in the confusing melee of aircraft it is impossible to say for certain who fired the fatal shots at von Osterroht, or who wounded the other pilot. Two of the Naval pilots felt certain that they had seen their fire hit home, but that is as far as it goes. Manfred von Richthofen had once been one of von Osterroht's observers in the days before he became a pilot. Breadner received the DSC shortly after this day's actions. In 1926, while attending RAF Staff College, he recorded;

'I was attached to 3 Naval Squadron, stationed first at Bertangles and later at Marieux, and worked with No 22 Wing, RFC. The squadron was equipped with Sopwith Pups armed with one Vickers gun firing through the propeller. Our duties consisted mainly of offensive patrols and escorting bombers and reconnaissance squadrons working over an area extending from the Scarpe to St Quentin. Offensive patrols were usually carried out by flights of five machines, and during this period they were performed at altitudes of between 12,000 and 16,000 ft. Their effectiveness during the spring months was marred to a great extent by the Pups' Vickers guns freezing in the air. On many occasions when Huns

All three of Shook's Pup victories came in N6200, which is seen here at Bray Dunes with fellow 'Naval 4' ace Flt Sub-Lt A J Enstone in the cockpit

Alexander Shook DSC scored three victories while flying Pups and nine more with the Camel

were attacked, they were unaware of our presence until we opened fire. After firing one round the gun stopped, and we had to break off the encounter to reload. We resorted to firing short bursts at intervals in an endeavour to keep our guns in action, but to no avail.

'The Sopwith Pup was in many ways an excellent machine for offensive patrols. It was at its best in a dogfight at high altitudes, as it would turn short and out-climb stationary-engined aeroplanes. It was, however, too slow to overtake an enemy machine with its nose down, as it did not dive well. Further, its rate of fire was much too slow, and during an engagement this was in sharp contrast to the rapid rate of fire of the enemy's guns.'

There was further success for 3 Naval Squadron on the afternoon of 24 April when Travers, Malone and Casey brought down a DFW C V two-seater near Morchies on the Allied side at 1650 hrs. The machine was from *Flieger-abteilung 26*, but its crew was not as lucky as that of the Gotha downed the previous day. Uffz Max Haase was taken prisoner, ending up in Brocton prison camp in Shropshire, but his observer, Ltn Karl Keim, was killed. The crashed machine was given the RFC number G25.

'NAVAL 4' ARRIVES

24 April had also seen 'Naval 4' claim its first success with the Pup when Flt Lt A M Shook sent a Fokker D II down out of control over Ghistelles at 1010 hrs. It was his first of an eventual 12 victories, the initial three of which would be scored while flying Pup N6200.

Canadian Alexander MacDonald Shook was born in December 1888 in Tioga, Ontario. Aged 28 by the time he reached the frontline, he was older than most of his contemporaries in the squadron. Shook had initially served with 5 Naval Wing in 1916 flying Sopwith two-seaters, after which he became a founder member of 'Naval 4' in April 1917.

The unit had been formed at Cudekirke (Coudekerque), near Dunkirk, from 'A' Squadron of 5 Naval Wing in December 1916. Initially equipped with some of the wing's Sopwith 1¹/2 Strutters, 'Naval 4' had started to receive Pups by March 1917. In April it was led by its CO, Sqn Cdr B L Huskisson, to Bray Dunes, situated on the coast north of Dunkirk. Unlike the other RNAS Pup squadrons attached to the RFC

Pup (N)9899 *DO-DO* flew with both 3 and 4 Naval Squadrons, and claimed five victories with such aces as Arnold Chadwick, Albert Enstone and Alexander Shook at the controls

Although not an ace, Hubert Broad nevertheless scored a few victories while serving with 'Naval 3' before being wounded by a long-range shot fired by German ace Adolf von Tutschek on 11 May 1917. He later served as a test pilot for Hawkers during World War 2

on the Somme front, 'Naval 4' was to be employed escorting RNAS bomber aircraft, as well as flying offensive patrols.

The squadron's CO, Bertrand Huskisson, had been employed by the Vickers Aircraft Company as early as 1911, when aged just 18, and had entered the RNAS in 1914. He would later become a wing commander, and holder of the DSC, *Legion d'Honneur* and *Croix de Guerre avec Palm*.

24 April had also seen No 54 Sqn's Capt J C Russell score an out-of-control victory over an Albatros D III north-east of St Quentin at 1930 hrs. His combat report is of interest, as it describes Russell making use of the sun to attack the German. One of Russell's pilots saw his fire hit the engine and then rake the rest of the machine.

'Naval 3' and '4' and No 54 Sqn were all in action on the 26th, Chadwick of 'Naval 4' being the first to see action in the middle of the afternoon when, south of Bruges, he claimed an Albatros D II out of control. Canadian Arnold Jacques Chadwick was born in Toronto in August 1895, and he too had joined the unit via the 5 Naval Wing route. Prior to flying Pups, he had had the misfortune to be shot down during a bomb raid on 2 October 1916, although he evaded capture and escaped to neutral Holland. On repatriation, Chadwick transferred to 4 Naval Squadron in April 1917, and this was his first victory.

Subsequently becoming a Pup ace, he more than doubled his score after the squadron re-equipped with Camels. But his luck ran out in July 1917 during a fight over the sea. Having been forced to ditch, Chadwick drowned before he could be rescued. His DSC was gazetted the following month.

The main Pup actions of the 26th began shortly after 1900 hrs when No 54 Sqn engaged several German single-seaters and claimed all three down out of control near Prémont. Capt F N Hudson, Lt S G Rome and 2Lt R M Charley were the claimants. This was Hudson's fifth victory and Charley's first. 'Naval 3's' Jack Malone and Francis Casey each shot down Albatros scouts north of Cambrai at 1915 hrs, Malone's being seen to crash – *Jasta* 3 lost a pilot in this area at around this time. Further north, Flt Sub-Lt C J Moir of 'Naval 4' claimed an Albatros D V out of control south-east of Dixmude.

It was 'Naval 3's' day on the 29th, with dogfights developing from 1030 through to 1115 hrs south of Cambrai. Joe Fall shot down an Albatros scout, Francis Casey got another in flames, Nick Carter and Hubert Broad each claimed 'smokers' and Lloyd Breadner a D III out of control. Hubert Broad, who would later become a well-known test pilot, was flying Pup N6203, which would subsequently see action with the Seaplane Defence Flight at St Pol.

On the last day of April, No 66 Sqn was first into action, Lt C C S Montgomery forcing an Albatros scout to land near Vitry at 0700 hrs. J O Andrews claimed an Albatros two-seater out of control between Fresnes and Brebières at 0845 hrs, and this time his victory was counted

– it was his first in a Pup, and his eighth overall. Forty-five minutes earlier, Lt G A Hyde MC of No 54 Sqn had claimed an Albatros scout out of control over Walincourt. Flt Sub-Lt L F W Smith of 'Naval 4' claimed another Albatros out of control east of Nieuport at 1245 hrs for his first victory.

Langley Frank Willard Smith came from Chicago, Illinois, although he was actually born in Philipsville, Province of Quebec, in August 1897. Having joined the Royal Navy, he learnt to fly at the Curtiss Flying School in Newport News, transferring to the RNAS in September 1916 and gaining his Royal Aero Club licence (No 3998) in December. Interestingly, he also gained a special Royal Aero Club Certificate (No 11) in February 1917.

Australian 'Naval 4' pilot Flt Sub-Lt C J Moir claimed an enemy aircraft out of control above the flooded area south of Nieuport at 1900 hrs on 30 April, although he was killed in action on 10 May near Zeebrugge on an escort mission while flying N6185 'A', which also displayed the name *ANZAC*. Moir was just 21, and he had received the French CdG just prior to his death.

Both the RNAS and RAF suffered the loss of experienced Pup pilots on 30 April. The first to fall was 'Naval 3's' ten-victory ace Jack Malone DSO, who was shot down by Paul Billik of *Jasta* 12 during a late after-noon sortie. It was Ltn Billik's first victory, and he would go on to score 31 (a total which included victories over several aces) before being shot down and taken prisoner on 10 August 1918.

A short while later Robert Oxspring was returning from patrol and flying into the setting sun. By pure chance he collided with a Bristol Fighter of No 48 Sqn and both aircraft begun to spin down, the Bristol (A7323) disintegrating in flames, killing both crew members. Oxspring was more fortunate. He clipped a haystack, which cushioned the final plunge, but in the crash the Pup's engine broke both his legs when it was pushed back into the cockpit. When soldiers came to help him, and offer him a cigarette, he refused, telling them that a lighted match and a petrol-soaked uniform and aircraft were not a good combination!

This incident ended Oxspring's war, and a Bar to his MC was gazetted in May. The citation stated that it was awarded for;

'. . . conspicuous gallantry and devotion to duty on several occasions. He has brought down three hostile machines, and in addition has forced

A seasoned fighter pilot, Capt R Oxspring MC of No 66 Sqn also missed out on ace status after being badly injured in a mid-air collision with a Bristol Fighter on 30 April 1917. Formerly with No 54 Sqn, he had claimed at least three Pup victories by the time of his flying accident

A line-up of Pups of No 66 Sqn's 'B' Flight at Vert Galand in early April 1917. A6152 '3' is in the foreground, A7323 '6' is next and A670 '5' beyond that. Capt Oxspring was at the controls of the latter machine when he collided with the No 48 Sqn Bristol Fighter on 30 April 1917

Capt W V Strugnell MC claimed five Pup victories with No 54 Sqn between 19 March and 11 May 1917, two of his successes coming in A7306

several others to land. He has at all times set a splendid example of courage and initiative.'

'Naval 3' lost yet another Pup and its pilot on 1 May, when Flt Sub-Lt A S Mather fell to the guns of Adolf von Tutschek of *Jasta* 12 and was made a PoW. He was flying Pup N6186, and it represented the German pilot's fifth victory in an eventual tally of 27. Evening up the score, Joe Fall claimed an Albatros in the same fight for his seventh victory. Elsewhere on the 2nd, Capt J O Andrews of No 66 Sqn claimed a scout out of control and Capt W V Strugnell of No 54 Sqn got a second east of St Quentin.

In the latter action, 'Struggy' Strugnell had engaged a German fighter which he had spotted on the tail of 2Lt G C T Hadrill's Pup, and he forced it to dive away. The fighter's dive grew ever steeper and then developed into a tight spin, but with other German machines engaging him, Strugnell could watch no longer. Hadrill was later shot down by German ace Werner Voss on 9 May, becoming his 27th victory. He spent the rest of the war as a PoW.

Armstrong, Whealy and Pierce added to their scores on the 2nd by downing an Albatros two-seater in flames over Bourlon Wood at 0700 hrs. This success represented the third victory for both Armstrong and Whealy, and it took Ed Pierce's tally to five. RFC and RNAS pilots shared victories not as fractions but as a full kill, whereas the Germans did not

Canadian H S Kerby DSC not only scored seven victories while serving with 'Naval 3', but went on to down two Gotha bombers in August 1917 as CO of the Walmer Defence Flight. He is pictured here (left) with Lt E D G Galley during his service as CO of No 4 Fighting School at Freiston

share claims at all. If two German pilots argued over who should get the credit, and the toss of a coin was not acceptable, the matter went to arbitration. A final single credit was then made official.

Francis Casey of 'Naval 3' claimed a D III out of control over Meovres at 1120 hrs, this success being his ninth, and final, victory. Casey received the DSC and went on leave, but in August, while 'stunting' over the airfield in one of the squadron's new Camels (B3805), he failed to recover from a spin and crashed to his death. The Camel was far less forgiving than the more docile Pup.

An hour after the combat over Moevres, but further north, Flt Cdr J D Newberry and F V Hall of 'Naval 4' engaged a two-seater. It was seen to break up in the air above Rosendael, near Dunkirk. A machine of FA 3 was lost near Dunkirk, and it may have been their victim. Both crewmen were killed.

That afternoon, J O Andrews claimed an Albatros out of control over Orchies, and at 2030 hrs 'Naval 9' downed a two-seater into the sea off Middlekerke. The successful pilots were Flt Sub-Lts H F Stackard and H E Mott. This appears to have been the aircraft of *Marine Feld- abteilung* 1, reported lost off Nieuport, Vzflgmstr (aviation chief petty officer) Bernhard von Wintersheim and observer Ltn z S Eberhard Stettner being killed. Mott (in N5188) was forced to make a landing on the beach east of Calais after this action, but returned the next day. This was Harold Francis Stackard's first successful combat.

Born in Norwich in March 1895, although when he joined the RNAS in 1916 he was living in Muswell Hill, London, Stackard had followed an unusual career path for a future aviator as he had served initially with the Royal Naval Division in the early months of the war. Serving in Antwerp and then Gallipoli in 1915, he then headed for France, and the RNAS, the following year. Although not a Pup ace, Stackard later achieved 15 victories scored with a combination of Pups, Triplanes and Camels. He also survived the conflict.

Harold Kerby claimed two out-of-control victories on 6 May, one being shared with 'Army' Armstrong. On the 7th, No 66 Sqn's J O Andrews and Lt P G Taylor each forced an Albatros D III to land in German territory during the afternoon. That day's third claim fell to squadronmate 2Lt A Bell-Irving, who also sent a D III spinning down out of control. Angus Bell-Irving was a cousin of the famous Bell-Irving brothers of Canada – there were six of them in total, three of whom were pilots in the RFC. Angus would win the MC later in the year, and become a flight commander with a victory tally of two plus two more damaged.

Australian Patrick Gordon Taylor had been born in the Sydney suburb of Mosman in October 1896. Still a student when war came, he joined the local militia and was later on the staff of the Australian Imperial Expeditionary Force as a lieutenant. Australia had a strictly enforced age policy for entry into its armed forces, and being only 18, Taylor was unable to transfer to active duty, so he applied to join the RFC, which he did in August 1916.

When the Author was co-writing *Above the Trenches* (Grub Street, 1990) with Chris Shores and Russell Guest, he wanted Taylor to be included in this account of World War 1 aces, but he was out-voted by his co-authors! He still maintains, though, that Taylor did achieve five victories. On 7 May 1917 – the day the great Albert Ball was lost in some confused evening fighting – Taylor recorded;

'Offensive Patrol at 13,000 ft, lasting two hours and thirty minutes. Six hostile scouts seen south of Oppy, approaching the frontline. Leader dived to attack, and I followed him down and attacked a Hun. A general dogfight followed in which I was separated from the rest of the flight. I attacked another Hun heading west, but lost him as he dived away. I waited down at 5000 ft and attacked an Albatros scout flying alone. The aircraft appeared to be hit and started to go down, but it seemed under control. I was unable to follow as I was attacked from behind by another Hun. Apparently, the Albatros I had attacked was seen to land by another member of the patrol. I saw an SE 5 diving steeply on the tail of a Hun. I started to return as fuel was getting low, picking up the rest of the flight over Arras.'

In his book *Sopwith Scout 7309* (Cassell and Co, 1968), Taylor expanded on this report, and especially on the final attack;

'. . . a spot of brilliant colour caught my eye down to the east. Another lone Albatros, flying east towards Hénin-Liétard. With little good light left, I sent my machine urgently down the slopes of air into a position to attack the Hun from behind. I found myself holding my breath, as though to breathe would alert him and he would be gone. Something told me this Hun had not seen me. The distance shortened as the familiar outline of the Albatros came in. I resisted the temptation to open fire too early. I watched his red fuselage and some other colours on the wing. The brilliant beast grew in my sights. Now I could see the pilot's head, above the streamlined fuselage of the Albatros.

'But suddenly I realised the gap was no longer closing. I had used up the height and he would be gone. I firmly pulled the firing ring, holding the Hun in the sights as the single Vickers began to pump out its rounds. Almost immediately the red machine reared up, as if the pilot had involuntarily jerked back the stick. A wild thrill went through me. I pulled out to avoid the Albatros as it fell over and headed down. It swept away steeply and, evidently with power full on, drew rapidly down into the east.'

Taylor was then attacked by a two-seater, whose gunner put several holes through his starboard wing. His attempted counter-attack was

frustrated when the German pilot dived steeply away and was soon out of range. The only other claim by a Pup pilot that day was by Flt Sub-Lt E W Busby of 'Naval 4', who sent a two-seater down out of control.

Two days later, on the 9th, 'Naval 4' again saw the bulk of the Pup action over Ghistelles. Between 0730 and 0800 hrs, Flt Sub-Lts A J Enstone and Langley Smith each claimed victories, the latter destroying a kite balloon and Enstone downing a two-seater. This was the first of 13 victories to be credited to Albert James Enstone, although only four of these would be scored while flying Pups. Born in Birmingham in August 1895, he had joined the RNAS in April 1916 and learned to fly at Cranwell, which was then a naval training school. When 'Naval 4' was formed, Enstone was one of its original pilots. His war flying would bring him the DSC and DFC.

At 1230 hrs on the 9th, Art Whealy of 'Naval 9' drove a Halberstadt scout down out of control. During the afternoon, No 54 Sqn's M D G Scott and M W B Cole each destroyed two-seaters near Séranvillers, while Lt E J Y Grevelink got a scout. The squadron was escorting FE 2s of No 22 Sqn on a vital photographic sortie at the time. It may well have been just one two-seater which crashed, as both pilots – and other observers – saw wreckage on the ground, and they may well have been looking at the same crash-site, although slightly different map references were recorded.

Grevelink had had his gun jam during the action, and having cleared it, he spotted a black and white scout heading towards a Pup. He attacked it at close range and saw it dive straight down. One of the FE 2 crews said that they had seen a black and white scout crash. Hans Klein of *Jasta* 4 was wounded in one hand (losing his right thumb) on this date, flying Albatros D III 794/17. Klein later won the *Pour le Mérite* and ended the war with 22 victories.

The son of an Army captain, Edward James Yzenhoed Grevelink came from Bedford, and had previously served in the Second Duke of

Three pilots of 'Naval 4'. In the centre is ace Albert Enstone DSC, who claimed four victories on Pups and nine on Camels – all with 'Naval 4'/No 204 Sqn. An original member of the squadron, he served in the frontline for over a year and ended up a flight commander. Enstone was also awarded a DFC to go with his DSC

Wellington's Regiment. Transferred to the RFC in July 1916, he went to France with No 54 Sqn in October of that year. Now he was 23 years old, and had less than one month to live.

As previously mentioned in this chapter, the Pup pilots did not have things all their own way on 9 May, for 2Lt G C T Hadrill was downed that afternoon by Werner Voss. Hadrill's Pup (A6174) came down intact, the fighter displaying the name *Canada* on the top wing. Its pilot actually hailed from Sevenoaks, in Kent, although he was working in Montreal when the war started.

The final Pup victory on the 9th took the form of yet another two-seater, which was brought down by Flt Lt A M Shook of 'Naval 4', in company with Langley Smith, who had now scored two of the day's claims. They saw it crash south-east of Ghistelles at 1715 hrs. Pup honours went to No 54 Sqn the following day when, at 1510 hrs, Capt R G H Pixley destroyed a two-seater. His fight with the German reconnaissance aircraft began at 9000 ft and lasted a quarter of an hour. The aircraft descended to 50 ft, before it finally crashed into a house. Pixley thought his foe had come down either at Lesdain or Séranvillers, south of Cambrai, although he admitted later that he had been so intent on the scrap that he had lost track of his position.

Heading west, still at low level, he was attacked by three German fighters, as well as by ground fire. Pixley managed to get across the trenches, only to have his bottom port wing buckle. The Pup (A668) turned upside down, smashed into a shell hole and was written off, but Pixley emerged with just a cut eyelid.

Also written-off that day were two of No 66 Sqn's Pups, shot down by Lothar von Richthofen and Karl Allmenröder of *Jasta* 11. Lt T H Wickett (A6178) was taken prisoner but 2Lt D Sheehan (A7303) was killed. With Moir of 'Naval 4' also lost, that made it four Pups destroyed for the day.

In the early evening of the 11th, six No 54 Sqn Pups shared in the destruction of another two-seater, which crashed near Walincourt at 1840 hrs. The German's opposition comprised Capt W V Strugnell, Lts O M Sutton, Grevelink, Scott, Cole and Maj C E Sutcliffe, who was not, as his rank might suggest, the CO, but merely a pilot holding a major's rank.

The squadron had been engaged on an offensive patrol when the pilots spotted what they noted as a large two-seater crossing the lines heading east. All the Pups took a turn at attacking the luckless German, and all from close range. The C-type went down in a spin, and 'Struggy' watched it crash. Thirty minutes later the patrol came across a flight of four German Albatros scouts near Le Catelet. In the engagement which ensued, the German fighters were scattered. Strugnell singled one out and fired as it dived away, then had the satisfaction of seeing it crash into a pond near Beaurevoir.

Flt Lt Ed Pierce made the only other Pup claim for that day when at noon he forced a two-seater to crash (or at least crash-land) at Noordschoote, on the Dutch frontier. He had recently left 'Naval 3', and was now with 'Naval 9', and this claim took his Pup victory tally to six. By 1918 Pierce was an instructor and flight commander with No 254 Sqn, flying coastal reconnaissance sorties in DH 9s.

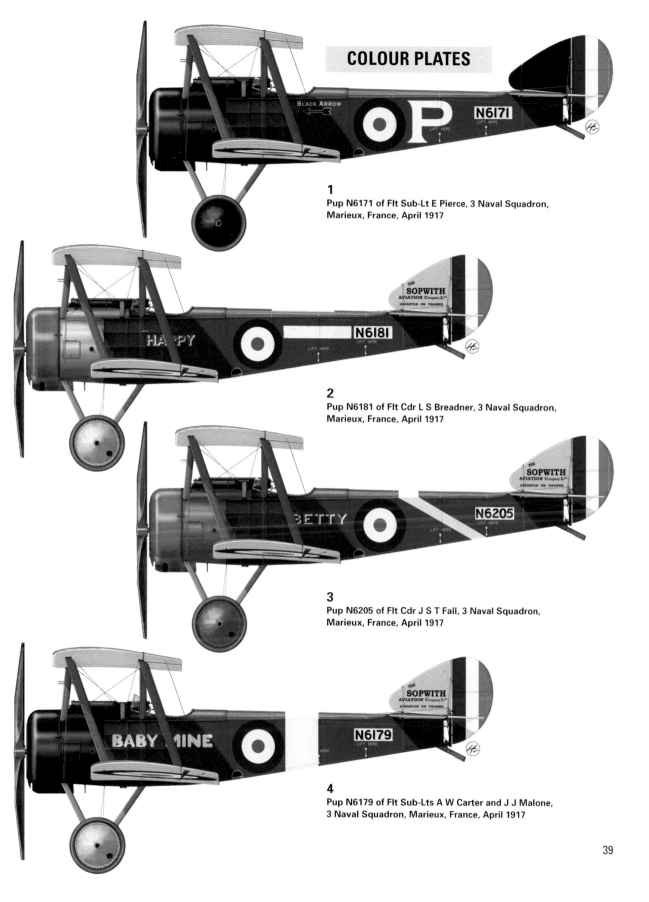

COLOUR PLATES

1
Pup N6171 of Flt Sub-Lt E Pierce, 3 Naval Squadron,
Marieux, France, April 1917

2
Pup N6181 of Flt Cdr L S Breadner, 3 Naval Squadron,
Marieux, France, April 1917

3
Pup N6205 of Flt Cdr J S T Fall, 3 Naval Squadron,
Marieux, France, April 1917

4
Pup N6179 of Flt Sub-Lts A W Carter and J J Malone,
3 Naval Squadron, Marieux, France, April 1917

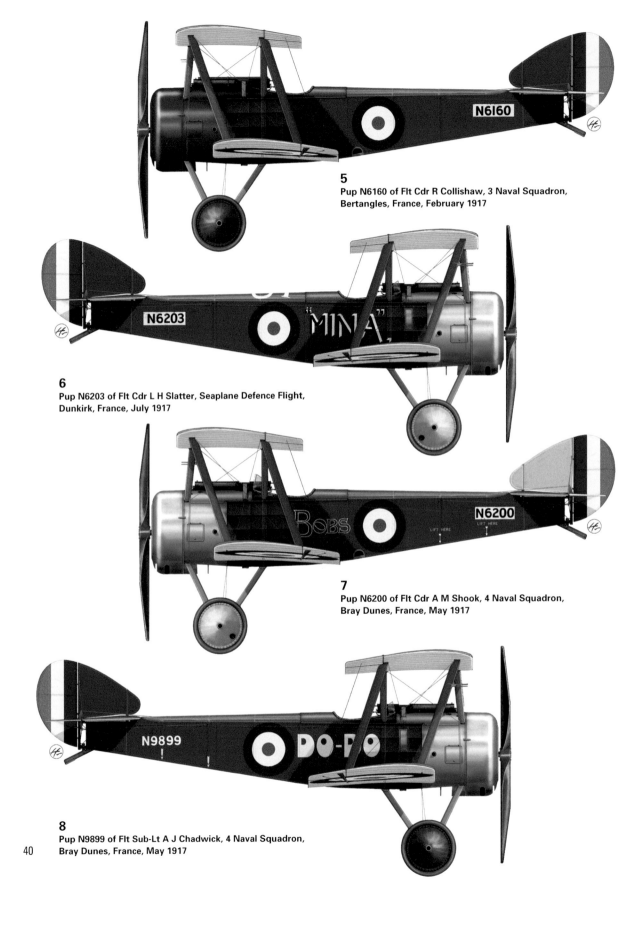

5
Pup N6160 of Flt Cdr R Collishaw, 3 Naval Squadron,
Bertangles, France, February 1917

6
Pup N6203 of Flt Cdr L H Slatter, Seaplane Defence Flight,
Dunkirk, France, July 1917

7
Pup N6200 of Flt Cdr A M Shook, 4 Naval Squadron,
Bray Dunes, France, May 1917

8
Pup N9899 of Flt Sub-Lt A J Chadwick, 4 Naval Squadron,
Bray Dunes, France, May 1917

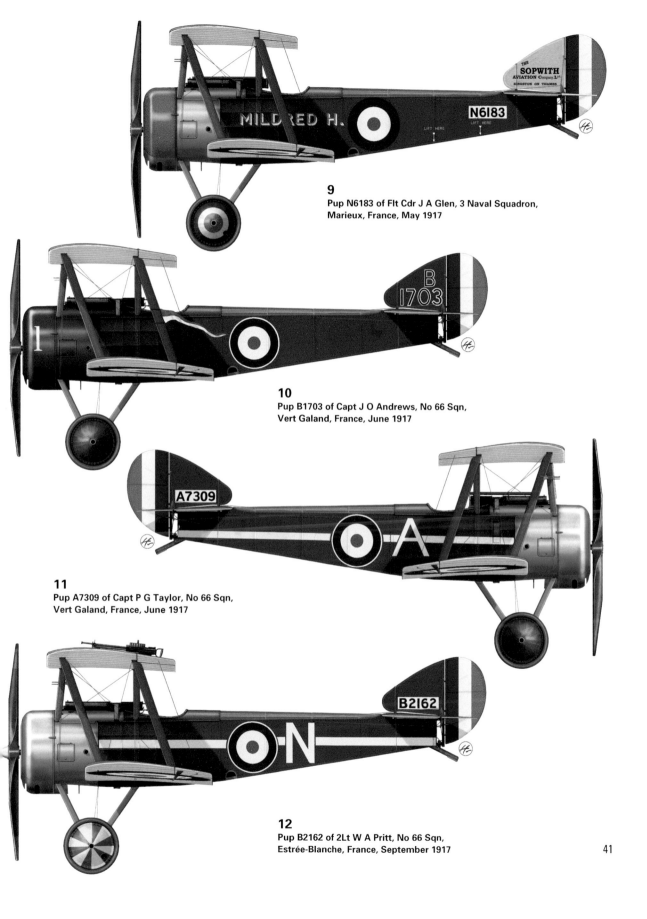

9
Pup N6183 of Flt Cdr J A Glen, 3 Naval Squadron,
Marieux, France, May 1917

10
Pup B1703 of Capt J O Andrews, No 66 Sqn,
Vert Galand, France, June 1917

11
Pup A7309 of Capt P G Taylor, No 66 Sqn,
Vert Galand, France, June 1917

12
Pup B2162 of 2Lt W A Pritt, No 66 Sqn,
Estrée-Blanche, France, September 1917

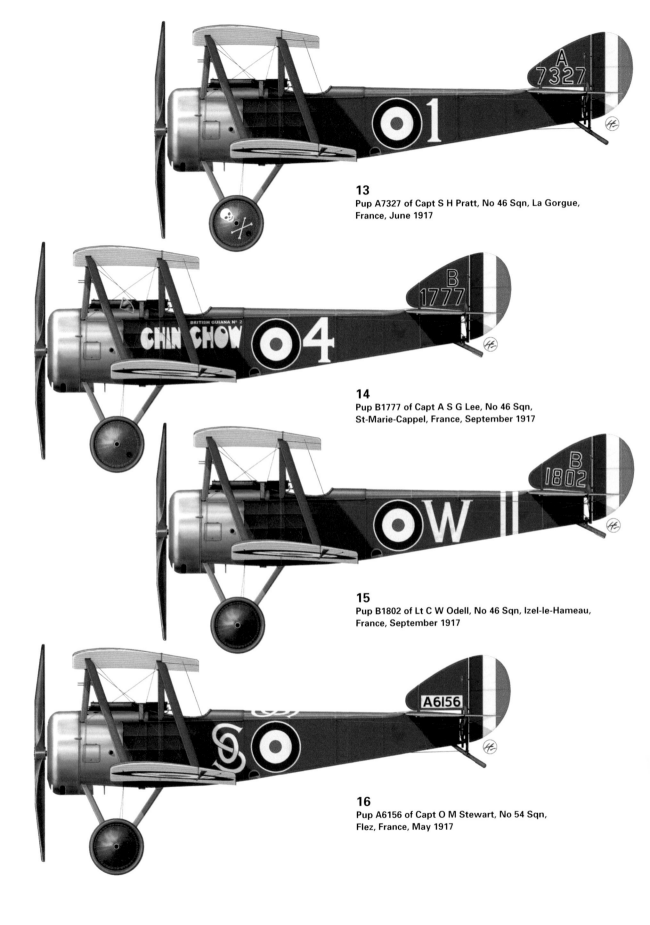

13
Pup A7327 of Capt S H Pratt, No 46 Sqn, La Gorgue,
France, June 1917

14
Pup B1777 of Capt A S G Lee, No 46 Sqn,
St-Marie-Cappel, France, September 1917

15
Pup B1802 of Lt C W Odell, No 46 Sqn, Izel-le-Hameau,
France, September 1917

16
Pup A6156 of Capt O M Stewart, No 54 Sqn,
Flez, France, May 1917

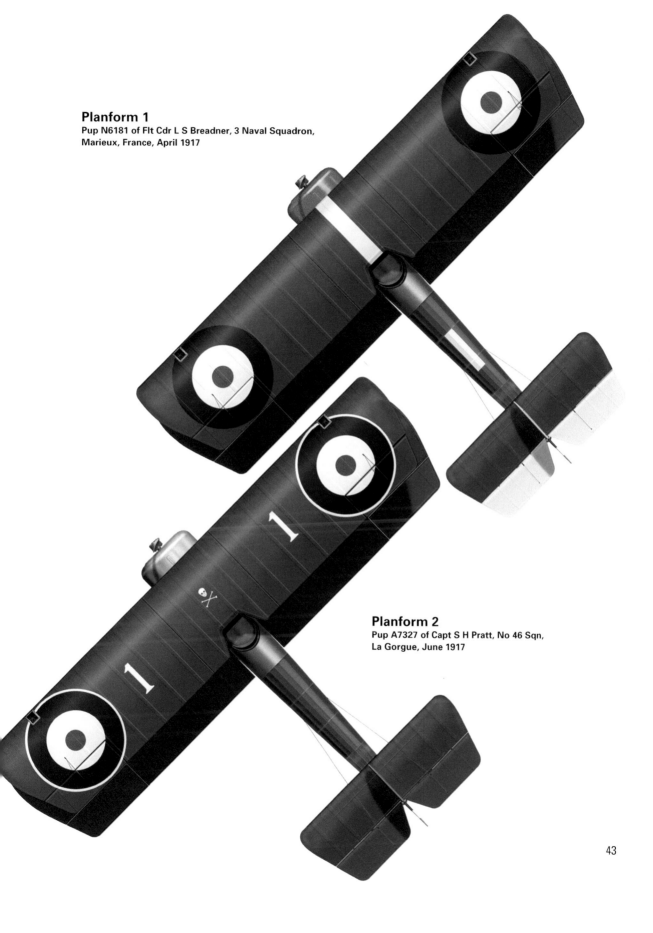

Planform 1
Pup N6181 of Flt Cdr L S Breadner, 3 Naval Squadron,
Marieux, France, April 1917

Planform 2
Pup A7327 of Capt S H Pratt, No 46 Sqn,
La Gorgue, June 1917

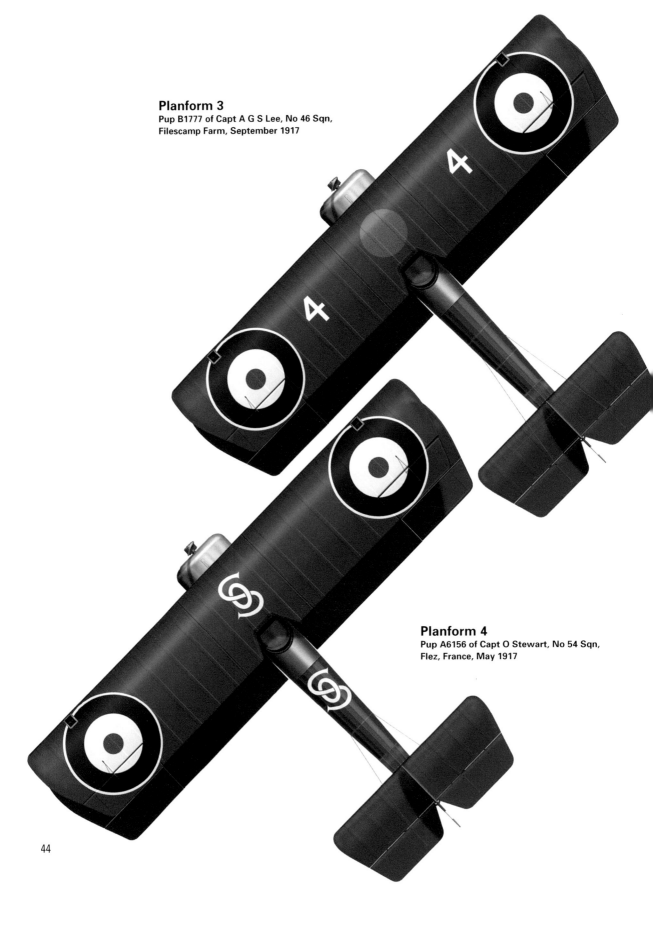

Planform 3
Pup B1777 of Capt A G S Lee, No 46 Sqn,
Filescamp Farm, September 1917

Planform 4
Pup A6156 of Capt O Stewart, No 54 Sqn,
Flez, France, May 1917

FIGHTING THE *JASTAS*

With 'Bloody April' beginning to fade from the memories of those who had survived it, the RFC and RNAS began to prepare for a summer of intense air fighting. Aerial engagements had continued into early May, and there was a flurry of activity involving the Pup squadrons that seemed set to continue for the rest of the month.

On the 12th, 4 Naval Squadron became embroiled in a large dogfight off the Belgian coast which lasted from around 0720 to 0745 hrs. Of the five pilots who claimed victories, four were aces or future aces. The opposition comprised a mixture of seaplanes, Albatros scouts and what was recorded or identified as Siemens-Schuckert D I scouts. These latter machines could easily be mistaken for Albatros or Nieuport scouts, having very similar configuration.

The D I was virtually a copy of the French Nieuport, with its sesquiplane layout – a very narrow chord lower wing – which necessitated a V-strut between the planes. Both aircraft also had rotary engines. The German High Command had requested that several designers make close copies of the Nieuport, the thinking being that they would achieve parity in combat with the Allied opponent. They certainly arrived in limited numbers on the Western Front at this time, but production ceased in July 1917. Like the Pup, it carried only a single machine gun. As far as is known, a few examples flew with *Jastas* 1, 2, 3, 4, 5, 7, 9 and 11.

The two naval pilots to claim D Is destroyed were future aces G W Hemming and A J Enstone, the latter doubling his score and Hemming opening his account. Geoffrey William Hemming, who was born in Worcester in April 1898, was a founder member of 'Naval 4'. He would gain three victories with Pups, three more on Camels and win the DSC and CdG. Both men made their claims against aircraft encountered some way off the coast of Zeebrugge, and at least one of the German scouts crashed into the sea.

Closer to shore, Langley Smith saw the Albatros D III that he had attacked crash into the sea as well. A M Shook also shot down a seaplane into the water, and Flt Sub-Lt E W Busby saw a second seaplane crash into the sea apparently out of control off Blankenburghe.

Flt Sub-Lt G W Hemming DSC of 'Naval 4' scored six victories in total, three of them on Pups

45

It would be good to be able to tie up these actions with casualties suffered by the Marine units, but as most known German loss records list only airmen killed and sometimes wounded, and not aircraft destroyed, this is difficult to do. If indeed the Germans lost between three and five aircraft in the sea of Zeebrugge, then all the pilots and aircrew not only survived but were also rescued.

Unfortunately, there are no timings available for claims by Marine *Jasta* Nr 1, which saw action off the coast that day, and their successes for this date do not help clear up the picture. Ltn z S Theo Osterkamp claimed a Sopwith off Ostende for his second victory (of an eventual 32), while Ltn z S Gotthard Sachsenberg was credited with a Pup for his third victory (of a final 31). RNAS losses in this area on this day were a Sopwith Triplane of 'Naval 10' and, as noted in some records, a 'Naval 4' Pup, although nothing is known of the latter.

Two hours later, at 0920 hrs, 9 Naval Squadron possibly got a two-seater off Nieuport, while the only RFC Pup pilot to score on the 12th was Mortimer Cole of No 54 Sqn – he shot down a two-seater between Sailly and Cambrai at 1100 hrs. The following day, J O Andrews claimed a D III out of control, and 'Morty' Cole got his fourth official victory on the 14th, although he is thought to have shared in another at some stage. He had been well to the fore since his arrival at No 54 Sqn in April, but his luck ran out on 26 May when he ran foul of Werner Voss, who shot him down on his 30th victory. Wounded in the thigh, Cole crashed into a shell hole in the British frontlines and managed to scramble into another, from which he was later rescued by soldiers. But his Pup (A6168) was a total write-off. Cole died from a heart attack in February 1947 in Minehead, aged 50.

Pup pilots did not achieve any further combat successes until 20 May, although they did suffer some casualties in their ranks. 'Naval 3' endured the worst attrition during this period, with Flt Sub-Lt H S 'Sport' Morton being brought down by Adolf von Tutschek of *Jasta* 12 on the 4th and Flt Sub-Lt John Bampfyde-Daniell falling victim to Vzfw Robert Riessinger, also of *Jasta* 12, one week later. Bampfyde-Daniell, who was made a PoW, was the first of Riessinger's four victories, two of which were Pups. Von Tutschek also accounted for 'Naval 3's' Flt Sub-Lt H S Broad on the 11th, although this victory was not so clear-cut.

Heading back to the British lines after a patrol, Broad had German fighters closing fast behind him, forcing the Pup pilot to keep on turning his head to keep an eye on his pursuers. Von Tutschek, who no doubt saw the frontlines approaching, fired off a long-range shot just as Broad looked round again. In doing so he had opened his mouth and a single bullet went into it and

'Naval 3's Flt Sub-Lt H S Broad was flying this Pup (N6162) on 11 May 1917 when he was wounded by a bullet entering his mouth as he looked back at a pursuing Albatros scout. Note the apparent white outer circle on both sides of the wheel covers

exited under his chin. Understandably, Broad quickly went into a spin, heading down and away, and managed to get across the lines to force-land near Bapaume. Von Tutschek, seeing the Sopwith spinning down towards the British lines, was convinced he had got his man. He returned home to be credited with his seventh victory. On the 14th Flt Sub-Lt W R Walker also failed to return.

On the 20th Len Rochford of 3 Naval Squadron, who had returned from leave four days earlier to find 'his' Pup (N6207) had been lost while being flown by 'Sport' Morton, claimed a D III out of control north-east of Bullencourt in N6461. Rochford recalled;

'On crossing the lines, we split up into twos and I paired with Wally Orchard. This idea of flying in pairs was Lt Col Vessey-Holt's, and it was supposed to enable the flight to cover a wider area in their search for enemy aircraft. Its disadvantage became apparent when a pair ran into a much larger force of enemy aircraft. I saw six Albatros scouts behind and below me near Bullencourt, and I attacked one of them without effect, so I then climbed in a westerly direction to gain height again. The Albatros followed me, firing at long range. After a while I returned and, finding them still near Bullencourt, I dived on one, fired a short burst and he immediately heeled over sideways and fell out of control.

'I found the "Archie" very accurate on my way home, and after landing at Marieux, we discovered that one of my Pup's former-ribs had been broken by a piece of shrapnel.'

'Naval 3' was also using an advanced landing ground (ALG) at Fremicourt so as to be nearer to the frontlines in order to be able to scramble standby aircraft to intercept German two-seaters spotted working near or over the trenches. This was a fairly new innovation for fighter squadrons, with No 40 Sqn RFC using Mazingarbe as an ALG whilst operating in just the same role with its Nieuport scouts.

No 66 Sqn claimed two German aircraft damaged on the 22nd, and 2Lt T C Luke of the same squadron sent a two-seater down out of control on the 23rd. Thomas Carlyon 'Sammy' Luke, who was born in Plymouth in July 1892, had earlier been a motorcyclist with the Royal Engineers. This was his first victory, and he would gain three more on Pups before being wounded while achieving his fourth on 28 July. Luke subsequently received the MC, and in the summer of 1918 returned to fly Camels with No 209 Sqn, gaining two more victories by war's end.

Despite Luke's success on 22 May, the day was to belong to 'Naval 3', whose pilots claimed four Albatros scouts in the early afternoon near Bourlon Wood. Three of these fell to aces Joe Fall, Jimmy Glen and Lloyd Breadner, while the fourth was claimed by Wally Orchard, who shared his victory with an FE 2 observer from No 18 Sqn. Technically speaking, Jimmy Glen was not yet an ace, as this was in fact his first of 15 victories. He would claim a further four in Pups and the rest in Camels.

Fellow naval ace James Alpheus Glen was yet another Canadian from Ontario, where he had been born in June 1890. Awarded the DSC and Bar and the CdG for his exploits in World War 1, he was to remain in the RAF post-war, and later spent time attached to the RCAF. Glen died in England in 1962.

Things hotted up for the Pup units in the final week of May, No 54 Sqn aces Oliver Stewart and Oliver Sutton claiming two victories on the 24th.

Although No 66 Sqn destroyed another aircraft on this day, it also lost one of its flight commanders when Capt L H Smith was forced down and made a PoW. He later escaped into Switzerland in December.

Oliver Sutton's was not the sort of victory one would choose everyday, however, as Stewart's combat report indicates;

'0810 hrs, Prémont, 18,000 ft, Sopwith Pup A6183, Albatros scout painted greyish, buff colour. Four single-seater hostile aircraft were attacked by the patrol, Lt Sutton engaging one nose on. Both machines flew straight at each other, and at the last moment, to avoid collision,

Pup A6194 of No 66 Sqn was brought down by a German two-seater on 24 May 1917, its pilot, Capt L H Smith, being captured, although he later escaped to Switzerland. Marked with the number '4' below the cockpit, the aircraft is seen here with Ltns Haugg and Kellein of FA48b, who were credited with downing the Pup near Noyelles-sous-Lens

Capt Oliver Stewart MC of No 54 Sqn poses with his distinctively marked Pup at Flez in June 1917. This was the third of the ace's Pups to feature his monogram, his first machine being serialled A6156 and a second A6211

Lt Sutton did a right-hand climbing turn but was just too late and hit the hostile aircraft with his right-hand top plane, tearing away the leading edge at the tip for nine inches, cracking the main spar and stripping off a large piece of fabric. Lt Sutton brought his machine back and landed safely on his own aerodrome. The hostile aircraft was seen by 2Lt M C McGregor to break into pieces and fall.'

The Author was in touch with Oliver Stewart in the mid-1960s, and asked him about Sutton's action that day. He recalled;

'On 24 May I was leading an offensive patrol with Oliver Sutton as sub-leader. In a dogfight, Sutton collided with one enemy aircraft and had about a foot cut off his starboard top wing. He managed to get back. I believe the event was reported in the press, and gave rise to the story that RFC pilots were using ramming as a deliberate tactic. It was, of course nothing more than an unintended collision, but it showed how news gets distorted during war.'

A NEW BRITISH ACE

On 25 May Capt S H Pratt scored his third victory (and the first in a Pup) when he sent an Albatros scout down out of control. Stuart Harvey Pratt was born in June 1893 and lived in Streatham Park, London, where his father ran a large furnishing store. He attended the University of London until 1910 and was an articled clerk to a London firm of chartered architects between 1911 and 1914. Serving with the Royal Fusiliers as a second lieutenant, Pratt was wounded in France, then transferred to the RFC in June 1916. Once trained as a pilot, he was posted to No 46 Sqn in August 1916.

The unit was operating Nieuport two-seaters at this stage, and Pratt and his observers scored two victories in February and March 1917. The pilot of the first was German ace Ltn Hans von Keundell, newly appointed leader of *Jasta* 27, and a man who had already gained 11 victories with *Jasta* 1 between August 1916 and January 1917. Pratt's observer in this action had been 2Lt Geoffrey Bryers, and von Keundell's

Nieuport 12 crews of No 46 Sqn pose for a group photograph prior to the unit's re-equipment with Pups. The pilot seated fourth from the left is Lt S H Pratt, who, with his observer Lt G Bryers (standing extreme right), helped shoot down Ltn Hans von Keundell, leader of *Jasta* 27, on 15 February 1917. Pratt claimed a further five victories with No 46 Sqn while flying the Pup

Capt Pratt's Pup A7327 '1', which featured a skull and crossbones on its wheel covers. The ace claimed all five of his Pup victories with this aircraft between 25 May and 17 June 1917

Pup A7348 '3' shares hangar space with Capt Pratt's A7327, easily identified by its unique wheel covers!

Albatros D III 2017/17, which was also attacked by a Nieuport scout of No 1 Sqn, was designated G11 as it fell inside British territory. Once the squadron re-equipped with Pups, Stuart Pratt became a flight commander in April 1917, and he would score another five victories to take his overall score to seven.

For some unknown reason, while working on *Above the Trenches* the authors missed including Pratt in their list of British aces. This may have been because in some records he is shown as S W Pratt, or because his first two claims were on two-seaters. Nor did his name come up before the men who approve decorations, for Capt Pratt received only a solitary Mention in Despatches for his work. The Author is pleased to help put the record straight by including him now in the ranks of British World War 1 aces.

Returning to England in June 1917, Pratt served with No 112 Home Defence Squadron. On 12 August he tried to engage a Gotha bomber raiding England but his guns jammed after 50 rounds and he had to break off. He was flying Pup B1773, and it was in this aircraft that on 31 August 1917, during gunnery practice at Herne Bay, he crashed and was seriously injured. Having lost his right eye and left foot in the accident, Pratt was invalided out of the service due to ill-health in December 1918 and put onto the retired list the following June. He lived in Sutton, Surrey, after the war, and in 1941 he volunteered for duty with the RAF Volunteer Reserve as a flight lieutenant with the Air Training Corps.

Flt Sub-Lts Langley Smith, Arnold Chadwick, E W Busby and G M T Rouse of 'Naval 4' attacked a Gotha bomber north of Westende at 1830 hrs on 25 May. Operated by the 13th *Kampfstaffel* of KG 3, the

Gotha crashed into the sea with the loss of its three-man crew, Ltns Willy Neumann and Werner Scholz and Oblt (observer) Manfred Messerschmidt gen von Arnim.

Earlier that same day, 'Naval 4's' Flt Sub-Lt S E Ellis had destroyed an Albatros D III south-east of Ghistelles. This was the first of two Pup victories for Ellis, which, with three later Camel claims, made him an ace. Canadian Sydney Emerson Ellis, who was born in Kingston, Ontario, in January 1896, had joined the RNAS in August 1916. Like a number of Pup aces, he too fell victim to the Camel's unforgiving handling characteristic, crashing to his death on 4 July 1917.

The RFC Pups added two more out-of-control victories on 25 May, Pratt hitting an Albatros scout and the second fighter being credited to 2Lt F A 'Long'Un' Smith of No 66 Sqn. The latter officer is not to be confused with Capt L A Smith, who, as mentioned earlier, had been shot down the previous day in Pup A6194 'A'. L A Smith's Sopwith Scout represented the fourth of 15 victories claimed by Ltn Julius Schmidt of *Jasta* 3.

'Long'Un' Smith was Australian Gordon Taylor's deputy leader at the time of this engagement on 25 May, and he had a red streamer attached to the tail of his Pup to denote his status in the flight. Taylor recalled in his autobiography that during the course of the dogfight he had spotted Smith in trouble with an Albatros scout and gone to his aid. There was no time to make a stealthy approach, so Taylor dived straight in. The German pilot was alive to the threat and, far from intimidated, did not half-roll and dive away, but turned to engage the Australian, spraying the new arrival with tracer fire. Taylor quickly side-slipped and then began a steep circle to enable him to take stock of the situation.

The Albatros was painted red with black and white checks on its fuselage, and Smith engaged him again and the German pilot started a good demonstration of combat flying. He had, according to Taylor, a nasty trick of flicking his machine around and hosing with his guns – something he had never previously experienced from an Albatros pilot. He seemed finally to run out of ammunition and headed east. On landing, Smith was enraged at the amount of damage the German had inflicted on his Pup. It was holed like a sieve, yet he had not been hit – a fact, Taylor noted, Smith seemed to ignore!

The following day, Lt C C S Montgomery of No 66 Sqn encountered some Albatros machines near Drury early in the morning, forcing one to land and damaging another. Just over an hour later, at 0845 hrs, Chadwick and Enstone of 'Naval 4' sent a two-seater down south-west of Furnes. Arthur Lee of No 46 Sqn nearly became a casualty himself during a patrol that evening, noting in his diary two days later that he had lost his sole companion and found himself alone. He became lost in reverie as he watched the evening sun sinking like a huge red ball towards the horizon;

'I was so wrapped up in it all that I quite forgot it was getting dark below, and that a freshening wind was keeping me over Hun land and, most important, that there was a war on. There was a sudden "rak-ak-ak-ak". My heart went into my mouth, in fact, practically out on to the dashboard – machine gun fire! Somebody was shooting at *me*! But from where? I looked behind. Nobody there. Then again came "rak-ak-ak-ak", and now tracers flashing past. Close! I could smell them, a kind of

Wearing his home-made frost protection mask, Australian Gordon Taylor climbs aboard his No 66 Sqn Pup A7309 at Vert Galand looking like something from the *Planet of the Apes*. Capt Taylor claimed the first three of his five Pup victories in this aircraft between 7 May and 15 June 1917

Lt M B G W 'Morty' Cole gained four victories while flying Pups with No 54 Sqn before being shot down and wounded by Werner Voss on 26 May 1917. He was the German ace's 30th victim

burning phosphorus. And then a startling sting in the calf of my right leg as though somebody had wiped it with a red-hot poker. By George, did I jump!

'I banked steeply over, and there, not far below, going east, was a Hun two-seater, dirty mottled green, with black crosses edged with white staring at me from the curving top wings and the fuselage. The observer was still firing at me, his gun flashing, his tracers seeming to come right into my engine. Forgetting all the tactics I'd learned from wall diagrams at training units telling me that a single scout should never dive on a two-seater's observer, but get under his tail, I dived on him, took careful aim through the Aldis and pressed the trigger. I was about 200 yards away, I suppose, and 100 ft higher, and I began to overtake. My tracers and his seemed to be practically hitting one another. Then suddenly his tracer stopped.

'Through the Aldis I saw him apparently sit down, then slide out of sight. The pilot turned, saw me just behind, and shoved his nose down. The blighter dived so fast that although I chased him hell for leather, firing continuously, he left me standing. And then my gun jammed.'

Lee broke off and headed west in the darkening sky. His leg was hurting, but he could see Ypres, and the last of the light reflected on the two lakes Zillebeke and Dickesbusch, so he knew where he was. Lee also knew there were fewer trees around Dickesbusch, so he chose to make a forced landing nearby. He was able to take note of the wind direction from smoke drifting from guns on the ground. Missing a church spire by inches, Lee touched down about ten feet from the water, ran forward a few yards then tipped into a shell-hole.

Within moments he was being helped from his wrecked Pup, dazed from a bang on the forehead due to hitting the gun butt. Taken into a nearby dugout, Lee was given a shot of whisky and his wound was tended. He was not having a great time with his legs, for he had been suffering from synovitis of the left knee since March.

Another RFC pilot wounded on the 26th was 'Morty' Cole of No 54 Sqn, who had his Pup (A6168) so badly shot up by Werner Voss (for his 30th victory) that he too had to crash-land on the right side of the trenches. Although wounded, Cole survived the encounter, but was effectively out of the war. The third Pup casualty that day was yet another No 66 Sqn machine (A6186), which 2Lt C F Smith brought down behind enemy lines following a fight with *Jasta* 12.

On 27 May it was 'Naval 3's' turn to inflict losses on the enemy, Glen and Kerby each claiming an Albatros D III destroyed, while Nick Carter sent one down out of control. T C Luke and C C Sharp of No 66 Sqn each claimed out-of-control victories on the 28th, as did Flt Cdr J D Newbury and Flt Sub-Lt E W Busby of 'Naval 4', who combined to send down a two-seater over Ostend that evening. May closed with Grevelink and Sutcliffe of No 54 Sqn claiming out of control victories on the 30th, while 'Naval 9's' Fred Banbury, Harold Stackard and T R Shearer sent a two-seater down out-of-control over Ostend the following afternoon.

These successes did not come without losses, however, for on the 27th a No 46 Sqn pilot was wounded and on the 28th No 66 Sqn's Lt R M Roberts was shot down by Walter Blume of *Jasta* 26 and taken prisoner. Finally, Lt F W Kantel of No 54 Sqn was brought down and captured on the 30th after tangling with *Jasta* 6.

MESSINES AND NO 46 SQN

June 1917 was to see intensive operations on the Flanders front, with the Battle of Messines opening on the 7th. On the morning of the 1st of June No 54 Sqn engaged the enemy in a large-scale dogfight over Gonnelieu, Oliver Sutton claiming one Albatros out of control and a second shared with M D G Scott. Just prior to this action, Fred Banbury of 'Naval 9' had sent a two-seater spinning down over Westende.

On 2 June, No 46 Sqn had managed to send down three Albatros scouts out of control in the Menin and Houthulst areas. These were significant victories, because they were the first multiple claims made by the unit since it had exchanged its Nieuport 12/20 two-seaters for single-seat Pups. The squadron had been in France since October 1916, and had started to convert to the Sopwith Scout in April 1917. On 12 May No 46 Sqn arrived at La Gorgue airfield, which was situated on the banks of the River Lys (often referred to as a canal). The unit was commanded by Maj P Babington MC, who had been in charge since the previous summer.

Stuart Pratt had made No 46 Sqn's first Pup claim on 25 May, this victory taking his personal tally to three – some records show that the 2 June claims were the unit's first, while others state that a German machine destroyed on the 4th was also No 46 Sqn's first victory. But Pratt got the first in May, albeit an out-of-control claim.

Arthur Lee had only recently been posted in to No 46 Sqn, and being a very new pilot, he was relieved to find that most of the others were as foreign to the Pup as he was. As he recorded later, they were all happy to be on single-seaters, although they were still learning how to handle them. They were still getting used to 'stunting' – that quaint contemporary term for aerobatics – and some had not yet tried a spin.

Pup pilots of No 46 Sqn enjoy the summer sun at La Gorgue in early June 1917. They are, left to right, R Plenty, R Heath, S H Pratt, C A Brewster-Joske, F L Luxmore, C J Marchant, K W McDonald, G P Kay and F Barager. 'Bob' Kay was killed in a crash on 29 June 1917

Capt Arthur Stanley Gould Lee MC of No 46 Sqn downed all five of his Pup victories in B1777 during September 1917

Born in Nottingham in August 1894, Arthur Lee had attended Nottingham University pre-war before becoming a journalist. Upon the outbreak of war, he served as a signals officer in the UK with the Sherwood Foresters, before joining the RFC to become a pilot. Lee had flown a Pup in from No 1 Air Depot and found it a joy to handle. He commented that it 'had a smooth and willing engine, very sensitive control responses and appeared as eager as a young colt'. He compared it to 'riding Pegasus, the mythical winged-horse'.

Pratt got another out-of-control Albatros on the 3rd, while Lt C A Brewster-Joske crashed another. The latter had also got one of the three that had fallen on the 2nd. Clive Alexander Brewster-Joske was an Australian, born in Fiji in October 1896. Educated in Melbourne, he served with the British Army in 1915 as a junior officer, then as an observer with the RFC. He and his pilot had helped to destroy a German aircraft whilst flying a Morane Parasol with No 1 Sqn soon after he arrived in the frontline. By August 1916 Brewster-Joske had become a pilot and been sent to No 46 Sqn. He would achieve eight Pup victories.

The Pups of No 54 Sqn once again set upon an Albatros scout en masse on 3 June, six pilots helping to send it down out of control east of St Emile at 0645 hrs. Although the airmen involved – Capts Sutton and Pixley, Maj Sutcliffe and Lts Scott, Grevelink and Sheridan – were an experienced lot, they could not register a positive kill. That afternoon, Chadwick of 'Naval 4' made a more certain claim, shooting down an Albatros D V near Cortemarck at 1640 hours for his fifth, and last, Pup victory. His next six would all be in Camels, as his unit would soon to be swapping its equipment.

Former artillery officer Capt Pixley of No 54 Sqn was himself brought down the next day (in B2151) by Werner Voss – he represented the German's 32nd victory. Twenty-four-year-old Old Etonian Reginald Pixley was killed. He had just been awarded the MC for 'conspicuous gallantry and devotion to duty', the citation adding;

'He attacked a hostile balloon with three other pilots and, remaining after they had left, finally sent it down in flames. He has assisted in bringing down several hostile machines, and has done good work throughout.'

The 4th saw several more successful encounters, with two enemy aircraft being destroyed by Nos 46 and 66 Sqn and one each by No 54 Sqn and 'Naval 4'. The two gained by No 46 Sqn were both Albatros D IIIs, one being credited to Lt F L Luxmore and the other to 2Lt C Courtneidge. Fran-

This line-up photograph of No 46 Sqn Pups at Bruay includes the machine (A7348) in which Lt C Courtneidge ditched in the Channel while flying to England on 10 July 1917

cis Luxmore never became an ace, but he gained much experience on fighters. Post-war, during operations in Iraq, he won the DFC. Charles Courtneidge was the brother of the famous stage-star Cicely Courtneidge, while his father Robert had produced the famous *Arcadians* on stage.

Lt F J Morse of No 54 Sqn had claimed a two-seater out of control at 0625 hrs on the 4th, while

Flt Sub-Lt S E Ellis had gained 'Naval 4's' solitary victory (an Albatros D III), and his first success, east of Dixmude two hours later.

Sydney Emerson Ellis was born in Kingston, Ontario, on 15 January 1896 and had joined the RNAS in August 1916. He would gain five victories (two on Pups and three on Camels) before being killed in July 1917 when he failed to recover from a spin. Finally, No 66 Sqn's 2Lt A B Thorne had scored both of the unit's victories over Zonnebecke on the 4th.

The following day No 46 Sqn claimed four more victories, Pratt getting an Albatros D III and Norm Dimmock and Luxmore a D V apiece. The fourth kill went to Capt R Plenty and 2Lt F B Barager, who shared in the destruction of a two-seater. Langley Smith of 'Naval 4' had burnt a balloon near Ostend at dawn, and Oliver Sutton claimed another D III out of control at 0700 hrs. In the late afternoon, Flt Sub-Lt H E Mott of 'Naval 9' set a two-seater on fire off Ostend, and during the early evening Enstone of 'Naval 4' destroyed a German machine north-east of Nieuport to score his fourth victory, and his last with Pups.

'Naval 11' operated Pups for a short time in 1917, including N6475 '9' which was up-ended at Handschute in July 1917. It had previously served with both 'Naval 4' and '9', where it was used by S E Ellis and J W Pinder to score victories

Norman Dimmock's Pup B1727 '2' of No 46 Sqn. Note the name *NORMIE* beneath the cockpit

Both Enstone and Francis Casey were soon to receive DSCs for their prowess, the latter's citation reading, 'He has shown conspicuous bravery and skill in attacking hostile aircraft on numerous occasions, bringing down four machines completely out of control and forcing others to land'. Casey was also Mentioned in Despatches on 11 May and 6 July 1917. He had been an acting flight commander since early June.

Enstone's medal citation duly recorded that the recipient was, 'specially mentioned for exceptional gallantry and for remarkable skill and courage in repeatedly attacking and destroying hostile aircraft, more especially on the occasion of hostile bombing attacks on England.'

At noon on 6 June, a No 54 Sqn patrol encountered a large group of Albatros scouts while escorting FE 2s south-west of Cambrai. The joint combat report for Sutton, Stewart,

R M Foster, A L Macfarlane and M C McGregor makes interesting reading due to its conclusions;

'A very large formation of hostile aircraft was encountered and the abovementioned officers engaged and drove down numerous hostile aircraft, and each of these pilots claim definitely to have destroyed one hostile aircraft, but owing to the presence of many others, it was impossible in any case for them to follow the hostile aircraft down. The claims of these pilots are based upon the fact that, after very close-range fighting, the hostile machines gave indication of being completely out of control. Three hostile aircraft were observed by other pilots to crash during this engagement, but two locations of crashed hostile aircraft are within 3000 yards, which renders it possible that both pilots referred to the same machine. One hostile machine was observed to crash by Anti-aircraft Artillery.'

It would be good to check German losses and see who it was that had been shot down by No 54 Sqn, but it is not that easy. While historians can get a good understanding of British wartime losses in terms of both aircraft and aircrew, the German records are not so clear. A list of German airmen killed does exist, together with a partial one of those wounded and taken prisoner, but a register of aircraft losses appears not to have survived, assuming there was ever such a document. It is assumed that at some time during the war there must have been a record of aircraft lost, if for no other reason than to aid requests for replacement machines.

This Author would be delighted if a long-lost volume listing every German aircraft written off or seriously damaged between 1914–18 were to come to light, but that seems unlikely.

It is certain that No 54 Sqn was in action with *Jasta* 12 on 6 June, and in gaining its 'five victories', the unit lost two pilots, Maj Sutcliffe and Lt

There are two aces amongst this group of No 54 Sqn Pup pilots seen in mid 1917. These aviators are, from left to right, Lt S G Rome, Capt S H Starey, Lt F J Morse, Lt R M Foster DFC (16 victories, including one on the Pup) and Capt O M Stewart MC (five Pup victories)

Grevelink, who were both killed. *Jasta* 12 claimed two Pups, one by Hermann Becker for his first victory, and one by Vfw Robert Riessinger for his second success. Becker would go on to claim 23 victories by war's end, and while nominated for the *Pour le Mérite*, the Armistice came before it could be awarded. Riessinger's score was an eventual four by mid-June, but he did not survive the month. *Jasta* 12 did not record any losses, so either they had pilots who crashed or crash-landed without injury, or what the No 54 Sqn pilots saw was actually their own squadron-mates falling.

Future ace R M Foster, who was to become Air Chief Marshal Sir Robert Foster KCB, CBE, DFC post-war, made his only claim with No 54 Sqn during this engagement. He would score a further 15 victories on Camels with No 209 Sqn. Yet another Staff College student to record his war experiences in the 1920s, Foster wrote;

'Our CO initiated and encouraged liaison with other squadrons in the Brigade, with the result that pilots knew personally the members of other squadrons whom we had to help to protect. The personnel of the FE 2 squadron (No 18) which was daily escorted by us, were always in and out of our Mess, and there was complete understanding between the two squadrons. This cooperation on the ground resulted in excellent combination in the air, which in turn bore fruit in maximum efficiency with a minimum of casualties.

Future ace Capt R M Foster DFC (later Air Chief Marshal Sir Robert) gained his first victory with No 54 Sqn on 6 June 1917. He claimed a further 15 flying Camels with No 209 Sqn in 1918

'To illustrate the close touch between the two squadrons, on one occasion the FE 2s and their escort were attacked about 15 miles over the lines. The fight lasted some time, and finished at 500 ft or so from the ground, the culminating *piece-de-resistance* being the spectacle of the leading FE 2 forcing a Hun to dive through the roof of a house at high speed. At the end of the fight, however, the leader of the FE 2s realised that he had insufficient petrol to regain his height and cross the lines at a safe altitude. He therefore made straight for home, accompanied by his escort. It certainly must have been an amazing sight for the Germans to see five FE 2s, with five Sopwith Pups 200 ft above them, all in close formation, flying low so far behind the frontlines.'

During the afternoon of the 6th, 'Naval 4' encountered Albatros scouts and Siemens-Schuckert D Is between Dixmude and Handzaeme, Langley Smith destroying one D V and sending another down out of control. Flt Sub-Lt G W Hemming destroyed a Siemens and sent a second down out of control. Two other pilots then sent a two-seater down in a spin north-east of Dixmude. Harold Stackard of 'Naval 9' came off second best in this encounter, however, as his Pup (N6193) was badly shot-up, although he was not hit. His fighter was something of a veteran, having been with the squadron since March, and its various pilots had accounted for four German aircraft destroyed. Once repaired, N6193 served with the Manston War Flight until finally struck off in January 1918, worn out.

As previously mentioned, the Battle of Messines began on the 7th with an enormous explosion. A tunnel under the German trenches, which took five months to dig, had been packed with tons of ammonal. It was detonated at 0310 hrs, and the explosion was heard as far away as London. A massive artillery barrage then followed as British troops advanced to take the ridge.

Ready for the off, No 66 Sqn's 12-victory ace Capt John Andrews models standard cold weather flying clothing at Vert Galand. Such garments were crucial when operating at heights above 10,000 ft

Australian Capt P G Taylor MC of No 66 Sqn claimed all five of his victories on Pups between 7 May and 11 September 1917

Both Nos 46 and 66 Sqns featured prominently that day, Brewster-Joske and J O Andrews destroying a D III and a C-type respectively. Gordon Taylor of No 66 Sqn was credited with a two-seater sent down out of control, this being his second victory. In his book, Taylor detailed how he and his fellow Pup pilots had been instructed to keep German reconnaissance aircraft away from the battle area at all cost. This was done so as to prevent the enemy from seeing how far forward Allied troops had moved, and also to frustrate German attempts at artillery-spotting.

Taylor and Andrews encountered several C-types and drove them off. After the latter had scored his victory, he had to break off with a jammed gun and a faltering engine. Taylor, meanwhile, carried on leading the patrol and eventually drove down his own two-seater. He then attacked a car and sent it and its three occupants into a ditch. Only two soldiers escaped. Staying low, he shot-up a gun battery and troops in a village to provide an example of the ground attack operations that would soon be on the increase. That evening Taylor was told he had won the MC.

The 7th also saw No 66 Sqn lose a Pup to *Jasta* 30, with another shot up, while No 46 Sqn had an aircraft downed by Max Müller of *Jasta* 28w. Flt Sub-Lt J W Pinder of 'Naval 9' redressed the balance slightly in the late afternoon by sending an Albatros D V down out of control south-west of Haynecourt. This was John Pinder's second victory of an eventual 17, but the only one he scored while flying a Pup. His first had come two days earlier in a Triplane, and the rest would be in Camels. Pinder ended the war as a captain and flight commander, holding the DFC and Bar.

It was more than a week before the next Pup victories, although there were losses. On the 8th No 66 Sqn lost two pilots to *Jasta* 8 – one in a collision – with another damaged and one shot-up. The Battle of Messines, however, had been won, and the victory had been helped by ground-strafing fighter aircraft. Arthur Lee recalled his part in this offensive while attending the RAF Staff College in the 1920s;

'Although during this period contact with the enemy was frequent enough, combats were often annoyingly indecisive. This was, I think, partly due to ignorance and personal factors, and partly to frequent gun stoppages. An impression that still remains of these combats is the feeling of foolish impotence that enveloped one when the single, slow-firing Vickers had a stoppage in the midst of a dogfight. Later, with Camels, everybody felt much happier behind a pair of Vickers. From 20,000 ft down to 15,000 ft, Pups could hold their own with most enemy craft, but below that height they were generally outmatched. Unsophisticated pilots who allowed themselves to be manoeuvred too low in a dogfight became casualties.'

On 15 June, 2Lt T C Luke of No 66 Sqn destroyed an Albatros west of Houthem at 0900 hrs and Capt Andrews forced a hostile aircraft to land. Until now, RFC pilots had referred to German machines as 'hostile aircraft' in their combat reports, but they now started calling them 'enemy aircraft'.

Capt Pratt of No 46 Sqn added another to his growing tally, sending down a two-seater on fire over Ploegsteert at 1050 hrs. Flying with Lt G S Kay, his combat report records;

'While looking for an enemy aircraft in answer to a call from "J" Battery AA, two enemy aircraft were seen east of Lille going north, and later two

Pilots of No 66 Sqn relax at Vert Galand Farm in May 1917. Standing second from the left is Capt R M Roberts MC who was shot down by Walter Blume of *Jasta* 26 on the 28th of that month. Standing at the far right is Lt J T Lucas, while seated in the deckchairs are Lt F A Smith, Capt J O Andrews DSO, MC, Lt Cox and unknown. Finally, in the front row, again from left to right, are Lts C C S Montgomery, Morley, J T Collier and R M Marsh

enemy aircraft were spotted south of Armentieres. All four refused combat. Then one enemy aircraft was seen proceeding from Freelinghein to Ploegsteert at about 13,000 ft. Both Sopwiths dived, but Lt Kay's gun jammed after a few rounds. Capt Pratt fired about 200 rounds. The enemy aircraft then turned towards Lille, diving steeply. Capt Pratt lost sight of it. The enemy aircraft was seen to go down with much smoke by "J" Battery AA. Later, Capt Pratt attacked another two-seater enemy aircraft over Lomme, but was forced to return after firing a few rounds owing to a lack of ammunition.'

Two days later Jimmy Glen of 'Naval 3' got a DFW north-east of Ypres for his third victory and Brewster-Joske and Stuart Pratt each sent an Albatros D V down out of control over Lens for their fourth and seventh respectively. Pratt's tour was about to end, and he returned to England on 21 June.

There now followed another long period in which Pups failed to secure victories over France. It lasted until early July, and was partly due to RFC squadrons being sent further north to counter the threat of German bombers attacking England. Daylight raids on 25 May and 5 and 13 June, as well as a night attack on 16/17 June, had caused consternation to the civilian population.

While Home Defence units were doing their best, their equipment was not suitable, and with radar and radio location still a long way off in the future, visual sightings of raiders had to provide information about approaching aircraft. Once in the air, there was no way pilots could be guided to the raiders other than by searchlights, which were not overly reliable.

As an interim measure, some Pup units were sent to the Channel coast in preparation for further raids. No 54 Sqn went to Bray Dunes, No 66

Capt A S G Lee's Pup B1777 '4' bore the presentation titling *BRITISH GUIANA Nº 2* and was named *CHIN-CHOW* by its pilot. It is seen here at Hornchurch in July 1917. Lee subsequently claimed all five of his Pup victories in this aircraft between 4 and 30 September 1917

Sqn to Calais and 3 Naval Squadron to Furnes, where it was due to convert to Camels. Other units were about to re-equip too, 'Naval 4' exchanging its Pups for Camels and 'Naval 9' acquiring Triplanes. Although it remained at La Gorgue, No 46 Sqn would soon be involved in countering the daylight raids too.

Yet little happened, leaving battle-weary pilots based near the sea to enjoy a well-deserved spell of rest in the early summer sunshine – some even enjoyed a spot of swimming. In between, a handful of patrols were flown over the Channel, but the skies remained empty of the big Gothas.

No 46 Sqn moved to Bruay on 6 July following another raid against England two days earlier. The move came in time for them to oppose a big raid on London by 24 Gothas on the 7th, although they failed in their attempts to intercept the bombers. Within days the unit had been pulled back to Sutton's Farm, in Essex, in what represented another knee-jerk reaction to the German raids. The squadron's pilots were not unhappy about this turn of events, however, as Arthur Gould recalled. When the unit arrived at St Eloi, the pilots of 'Naval 8' laughed when they saw that No 46 Sqn was still flying Pups. But the RFC pilots had the last laugh when they were posted back to England!

Despite failing to engage the Gothas, Pup pilots saw action elsewhere on the 7th when 'Naval 3' caught a seaplane over the water north of Ostend at 1110 hrs. Len Rochford, Joe Fall, 'Army' Armstrong, Jimmy Glen and Flt Sub-Lt R F P Abbott combined to send it crashing into the water. Fall and Glen went after another seaplane, which also went down into the sea a few minutes later. Alerted to raiders heading for England, the unit had taken off to intercept the Gothas, but had instead run into six seaplanes at 10,000 ft, 25 miles off Ostend. Len Rochford recorded;

'We dived on them and Joe Fall attacked one, firing into him at close range. Then Armstrong and I followed a seaplane as it dived down steeply, emitting clouds of smoke, to crash in the sea near a German destroyer, which opened fire on us. Fall attacked another seaplane, firing about 150 rounds at close range until it heeled over, side-slipped and dived into the sea about a mile north-west of Ostend Pier, leaving a trail of blue smoke in the sky. A third seaplane was attacked by Glen from underneath, firing 150 rounds at close range. This one dived straight into the sea and sank almost immediately, only pieces of the seaplane remaining on the surface of the water.'

Only two seaplanes were actually shot down in this action, while the Pup flown by Flt Sub-Lt L L Lindsay developed engine trouble, forcing him to also come down into the sea. His lifebelt failed and he had to swim for it, although he was soon picked up by a French destroyer. An hour later 'Naval 3' was again airborne to intercept the returning raiders, although no Gothas were seen. Instead, the pilots encountered more seaplanes and Albatros scouts north of Ostend, these machines guarding the raiders' flightpath, as well as being on hand for air-sea rescue duties. Joe Fall shot down a D V in flames to take his victory tally to 11 on Pups, although it was to be his last while flying the type.

Len Rochford had also taken off on 'Naval 3's' second interception sortie of the day, although on this occasion he was flying a Camel which was afflicted by fuel pressure problems. He duly returned to base early.

Again, there are no German loss records to help identify the combatants. Two *Seeflug* Station Nr 1 crews were taken prisoner on the 9th, and they ended up in Kegworth prison camp, but whether they were among the crews claimed by 'Naval 3' – one of which would appear to have been rescued by a German warship – is unclear. Perhaps they were in the water for two days and only picked up on the 9th.

That evening 'Naval 9' was in action south-west of Haynecourt, Art Whealy sending an Albatros D V spinning earthwards, while Flt Cdr G E Hervey, and Flt Sub-Lts Mott and Pinder claimed another. Finally, a two-seater spotted nearby was attacked and shot down by Flt Sub-Lt J C Tanner, the aircraft crashing near Bullencourt at 1730 hrs. Minutes later Tanner himself became a victim when he was shot down by an the *Jasta* 4 Albatros flown by Gerhard Anders, who thereby scored his first victory. Anders later flew with *Jasta* 73, with whom he took his score to seven following six night victories over French bombers.

Tanner was reported to have died of his wounds, but he came down over Allied lines and was in fact killed in a flying accident in England on 1 August 1918.

Pup pilots finally caught sight of the elusive Gotha bombers on the evening of 10 July, when Spencer Kerby, Len Rochford and Harold Ireland spotted a formation of eight Gothas below them while patrolling off Middlekerke. They dived to attack, but as they did so they spotted more than a dozen Albatros scouts above and behind the bombers. This understandably distracted them, and Kerby decided the odds were too great and the Pups headed west as fast as they could!

Capt F N Hudson MC of No 54 Sqn shot a two-seater into the sea off Nieuport in the early morning of the 11th, this success being his sixth and final Pup victory. Although Hudson did not see it crash, the aircraft was later confirmed to have dived into the sea by RNAS HQ at La Panne, as well as by a Belgian coastguard.

No 66 Sqn's J O Andrews sent another down in flames near Henin at 1035 hrs that same morning, this too being Andrews' final combat claim, taking his score to 12 (of which five were on Pups). His victim may have been an aircraft from *Schusta* 9, which lost a crew in this area.

The following evening, squadron-mates Lts T V Hunter and E H Lascelles fought Albatros scouts north-east of Ypres, the latter pilot reporting one destroyed, while Hunter sent another down out of control.

This victory was the first of four on Pups for Londoner Thomas Vicars Hunter, and a fifth would follow on the Camel before he was killed in a flying accident in December 1917. He was known as 'Sticky' Hunter because he had lost a leg in France in early 1915 while serving with the Rifle Brigade. Fitted with a wooden leg, the only way he could get back into the action was in the cockpit of an aircraft.

13 July saw two more claims, one of which fell to No 66 Sqn's Lt Montgomery at 0620 hrs and the other to 2Lt R M Charley of No 54 Sqn, who

downed an Albatros at 1315 hrs. The latter represented Reg Charley's second victory, and his first since April.

On a negative note, No 54 Sqn lost Frank Neville that same day when he was brought down wounded by Ltn Gerhard Flecken of *Jasta* 20 and taken prisoner. Neville was the second of four victories for Flecken. Another near loss came on the 16th, when 'Sticky' Hunter had his aileron controls shot away in a dogfight. He somehow managed to get down safely on the right side of the lines, and he was flying again the very next day. Hunter was flying future 'ace' Pup B1760 on the 16th, and squadron mechanics had it repaired by the morning of 17 July.

That same day saw 'Naval 11's' Flt Sub-Lt A R Brown claim a D III out of control and his squadron-mate Flt Sub-Lt H E Airey down a two-seater south of Middlekerke. 'Naval 11' had been formed at Dunkirk in March and moved to Hondschoote in 11 July. It was disbanded on 27 August.

Capt R M Charley of No 54 Sqn claimed five Albatros scouts destroyed in the Pup between 26 April and 12 November 1917. The latter success, over a D V, gave Charley the distinction of being the last ace to score five victories with the Pup

Canadian Brown sent his victim down south-east of Nieuport at 1845 hrs while flying N6174. He would later gain fame for his actions in the late morning of 21 April 1918 during Baron Manfred von Richthofen's last combat. By then a Camel ace with the DSC to his name, he chased the Baron's red Fokker Dr I off the tail of fellow Canadian Wilfred May. The pursuit ended when ground fire brought the German ace down. This all lay in the future when Brown made the following entry in his log-book;

'17/7/17, 5.50 pm, Pup 6174, OP Ostend. I saw our AA south-east of Nieuport and went to see what they were firing at. I then dove on six to eight Albatros scouts. Opening fire on one, I got one burst in and he went down in a spin. My gun then jammed, and once I had cleared it I opened fire on another – I got about 50 rounds right into him and he went down out of control. My gun then jammed again. A Hun opened fire on my tail, so I side-looped and cleared the jam. Going over, I came out under his tail and got 20 rounds into him and he went down spinning. There were now no more Huns left. The AA was very severe coming back over. I was low, and my machine was hit in upper right plane by AA.'

Brown had recorded only about 85 flying hours at this time. In early September he made his first flight in a Camel, and he was not impressed. He wrote in his log-book, 'first flip on Clerget Camel. Do not like them'.

BATTLING ON

With fewer Pups now present on the Western Front due to the arrival of Sopwith Triplanes and Camels, the type failed to feature in any successful combats until the end of July 1917. Even then, the engagement was brief, and it was well into August before the next victories came. A number of Pup squadrons were also away from the immediate frontline in England on Home Defence duties, while others were in the process of transitioning to Triplanes or Camels.

Of the three RFC Pup units, No 46 Sqn was at Sutton's Farm, in Essex, No 54 Sqn was at Leffrinckhouke, near Dunkirk, and No 66 Sqn was at Estrée Blanche, south of St Omer. The latter unit's 'A' Flight commander Capt J O Andrews had recently become tour-expired, and the award of the DSO showed his worth in the recent fighting. The unit's CO was also leaving, O T Boyd's place being taken by Maj G L P Henderson, while command of 'A' Flight went to Capt Gordon Taylor MC. Three naval squadrons – 3, 4 and 9 – which had previously flown Pups were all now equipped with Camels, and 'Naval 11' was about to disband, leaving the RFC with the only operational Pups. 'Naval 3's' Len Rochford recalled;

'A trip to Wimereux provided me with my last flight in a Sopwith Pup for, by the middle of July, the Sopwith Camel had completely replaced our Pups. Although the Pup was a delightful little aeroplane to fly, the Camel was undoubtedly a much superior fighting machine.'

The new Sopwith scout had arrived just in the nick of time too, for RFC and RNAS fighter patrols were now generally out-numbered by hostile aircraft whenever they flew over the frontline. It was not so much that the *Jastas* were flying in combined groups, nor that the new Richthofen *Jagdesgeschwader*, or other temporary *Jagdgruppen*, were

No 46 Sqn's Lt C J 'Chaps' Marchant poses with his Pup at Filescamp Farm in September 1917

operating a lot more aircraft. German commanders did not find it easy to lead large formations of aircraft either, yet pilots seemed to home in on Allied activity above the lines and appear quickly to out-number the British. It might also be suspected that pilots returning from a bit of a drubbing in air combat tended to exaggerate the number of aircraft engaging them, human nature being what it is. Nevertheless, combat-weary British pilots felt that something should be done.

Some flight commanders in various squadrons had been suggesting that combined operations should be mounted to try and mass fighters against the larger German formations. Such requests normally fell on deaf ears, but quite out of the blue at the end of July the local Wing Headquarters gave approval for just such an operation. As a result, on 27 July Pups of No 66 Sqn, SE 5s from No 56 Sqn, SPAD VIIs of No 19 Sqn and some RNAS Camels and Triplanes met over Roulers, staggered down from 18,000 to 10,000 ft. Strangely enough, the Germans reacted, but were completely overwhelmed. Some fights developed, but the majority of German pilots quickly headed for the deck and home. Some were shot down, however, and 'Sticky' Hunter of No 66 Sqn managed to claim an Albatros D III destroyed over Ardoye at 1700 hrs. A solitary Pup from No 66 Sqn was shot-up by a *Jasta* 24 pilot, but its pilot returned safely.

With so many German aircraft turning for home at the sight of this formation, RFC squadron commanders felt vindicated in their assertion that patrols should be much larger than flight-size as a matter of course. The problem that faced wings was that while this could be managed, it caused too many gaps to appear in overlapping patrols, which in turn resulted in reconnaissance and artillery spotting aircraft being left vulnerable to German predators.

Pup B1779 of No 54 Sqn crashed at Furnes on 24 July 1917. A presentation machine, it displayed the dedication *PRESENTED BY THE NATIVES OF REWA PROVINCE, COLONY OF FIJI. FOR THE USE OF THE ROYAL FLYING CORPS, 1917.* Damaged in an dogfight, it had lasted just 17 days on the squadron

The next day it was back to normal, No 66 Sqn losing a Pup and pilot (later captured) on an early flight-strength patrol. A few hours later the squadron endured a violent encounter with several Albatros Scouts, again over Roulers at around 2000 hrs. It was as if the Germans had come up to avenge their humiliation of the previous day. Gordon Taylor led his flight down on to one bunch and managed to get into position on an aircraft from the inside of a turn as its pilot tried to out-manoeuvre the Pup. Taylor recorded;

'For a few moments I had him in my sights and got a good burst into the silver machine. Then I was horrified to see "The Ratter's" (Lt Boumphrey) Pup cutting across in front of me, also making for the Hun. I just escaped a collision by ramming the stick forward and slewing out of the way. I then saw the Hun going down, obviously out of control. "The Ratter's" Pup was there, but another Pup was in bad trouble, holding a tight turn while an Albatros hung above him. I went for this Hun, and was drawing a very careful bead on him, when I was attacked from behind. My quarry was so close that the ripping of his Spandaus cut like some blast from the heavens through the high note of my Le Rhône.

The rather spartan cockpit of a Sopwith Pup. The control column can be seen in the lower left corner of the photograph.

'The reaction, as usual, was instantaneous, my hand jerking my machine round even before the shock of the attack could consciously register. For a frantic moment I went through the effect of death in my cockpit. I knew that I had swept my machine out and the Hun had passed. I saw him, hauling up, tail on, climbing into the sky. Then he was suddenly obliterated by a flaming mass plunging down in front of me, trailing a column of black smoke. It was another Albatros. I couldn't reach him or do anything in time. Futilely, I shouted, "Look out, Sammy! Look out!" I saw tracer cutting into the Pup. It suddenly reared up, pulled over, and started to go down, west, towards out lines. The Hun did not follow. He turned away to the east and disappeared.'

Four machines landed back at Estrée, T C Luke being the missing Pup pilot. Although wounded, he got down safely and went into hospital – he also claimed one enemy aircraft sent down in flames. W A Pritt and F G Huxley also claimed one crashed, and four more were sent down out of control by Taylor, Hunter, E L Ardley and J W Boumphrey. The victor over Sammy Luke was probably Oskar Freiherr von Boenigk of

65

Looking more like a 15-year-old schoolboy than a 20-year-old ace, Lt Walbanke A Pritt MC claimed six Pup victories with No 66 Sqn between 28 July and 30 September 1917

In 1917, Ronald Graham DSO, DSC, DFC commanded the Seaplane Defence Flight at Dunkirk, which later became 'Naval 13'. Graham gained one of his five victories while flying a Pup

Jasta 4, who claimed a Sopwith at 2105 hrs near Moorslede. It was his second of an eventual 26 victories. Luke's own claim was his fourth. He was awarded the MC 'for conspicuous gallantry and devotion to duty in aerial combat', the medal's citation adding;

'On several occasions he attacked hostile formations and dispersed them, although they were in superior numbers, showing great dash and fearlessness in engaging them at close range. He has taken part in 35 offensive patrols, at all times setting a fine example of courage and devotion to duty.'

Luke's victim may have been the leader of *Jasta* 8, Hptm Gustav Stenzel, who had achieved four victories so far, two of them while flying in Macedonia in 1916. He was lost over Rumbeke, near to where the combat took place.

Mention of the shared victory by Pritt and Huxley refers to the first claim by Walbanke Ashby Pritt from Leamington Spa. Born in October 1897, he was still three months shy of his 20th birthday, but he looked even younger. Gordon Taylor put his age at more like 15, but his records show he was in fact 19. He owned a small dog named 'Dickebusch', after the famous lake which acted as a landmark on this part of the front. To make the dog a recognisable member of No 66 Sqn, Pritt painted red, white and blue roundels on both sides of the animal! Pritt would score five or six victories and win the MC.

THIRD YPRES

The Third Battle of Ypres – also known as Passchendaele – opened on 31 July 1917. It began with an attack on Pilckem Wood, and the battle would rage until November. RFC Pups were in the thick of it, engaged in fights at Langemark, Polygon Wood and finally Passchendaele itself, where more soldiers seemed to drown in the mud than were killed by shells and bullets.

August proved disappointing in terms of aerial victories for the Pup units, but things looked up on the 12th for No 54 Sqn. G A Hyde and F W Gibbes shared an Albatros driven down out of control, and H H Maddocks claimed another. That evening there was another daylight Gotha raid, with around a dozen bombers going for Southend.

Henry Hollingrake Maddocks, who was born in London in August 1898, had joined the RFC in June 1916. He would score four victories with the Pup and a further three with Camels before his service in France came to an end in February 1918. This first victory came just five days after his 19th birthday.

Once again the German seaplanes were out on 12 August, providing escort and help should any of the raiders come down in the sea. The RNAS Seaplane Defence Flight, equipped with Pups, was based at Dunkirk, and its pilots flew out north of Ostend to meet the enemy. Flt Lt P S Fisher, in company with Flt Sub-Lts R Graham and L H Slatter, shot down a Friedrichshafen FF 33L (No 1246) two-seat patrol/escort seaplane from *Seeflug* Station 1. Its crew of FlgMt Walter Paatz and Vzflugm Heinrich Putz were both killed.

Leonard Henry Slatter and Ronnie Graham would both become decorated fighter aces in this war, although they would not score all their victories exclusively on Pups. Both would gain high rank in the future

RAF. Slatter came from Durban, South Africa and Graham was actually born in Japan. They would end their careers as an air marshal and air vice-marshal respectively, Slatter with an OBE and the DSC and Bar, plus the DFC, and Graham with the CB, CBE, DSO, DSC and Bar and the DFC.

Capt Leonard Slatter DSC gained a victory with the Seaplane Defence Flight while flying a Pup. He also used the Sopwith Scout to damage a Gotha bomber at night

Leonard Slatter flew Pup N6203 *"MINA"* (N6203) whilst with the Seaplane Defence Flight. The fighter is seen here parked outside the hangars at Dunkirk, the Pup's distinctive 'S' marking being visible on the fuselage decking. Note also the two tear shapes on its tailplane

The evening of 12 August also saw Harold Spencer Kerby, formerly of 'Naval 3' and now engaged on Home Defence duties at Walmer airfield, in Kent, sent up with another Pup pilot to chase a lone Gotha which had bombed Margate and was returning to base. Kerby spotted eight Gothas of the main force being engaged by Camels from Eastchurch, so he climbed above the bombers and made a diving attack from the front. His fire resulted in Gotha G IV (No 656/16) going straight down into the sea some way off Southend, where it turned onto its back.

As Kerby circled the crash site, he saw a crewman clinging to the tail of the machine, so he flew low and threw him his lifebelt. He then tried to attract the attention of four destroyers nearby, but they failed to understand his signals and sailed on. Kerby was awarded the DSC, and this was his eighth victory scored while flying Pups. The crew of Uffz Rudi Stolle, Ltn Hans Rolin and Uffz Otto Rosinsky all perished, and only Stolle's body was recovered – washed up on the Belgian coast, it was buried at Gontrude. The aircraft was from *Kampfstaffel* 16 of KG 3. Kerby later recorded;

'The hostile aircraft were about 2000 ft above me when I got under them. I followed, climbing to 18,000 ft and attacked without result. I then observed one Gotha 4000 ft below the formation, but still flying with it. I attacked from the front and drove him down into water, where I observed him turn over. One of the occupants I saw hanging on the tail of the Gotha. I threw him my lifebelt and did two or three circuits round him and then returned to England. On my way back I observed four destroyers when at 6000 ft sailing towards Dunkirk. I fired three red Very Lights to try and get them to follow me back to the machine in the water, but they continued on their course.'

Back on the Western Front, Capt Stewart, along with 2Lts C G Wood and G Clapham, of No 54 Sqn destroyed a two-seater south of Middlekerke at 0730 hrs on 15 August. The next day, W A Pritt of No 66 Sqn made a name for himself in a lone attack on a German airfield. Flying low and shooting up the airfield, he then saw an Albatros D V

No 66 Sqn's Lt Pritt used Pup B2162 to claim his final two victories on 4 and 30 September 1917. The aircraft was fitted with a Lewis 0.303-in machine gun on the top wing in addition to its standard Vickers 0.303-in weapon

taking off. He sent it down to crash soon after it became airborne, followed shortly afterwards by a second Albatros that he also spotted taking off. Pritt was certainly an aggressive pilot.

Once, on a ground-strafing sortie, he saw what appeared to be a German staff car containing officers. He dived down on it in an effort to try and make its driver swerve into a ditch, but the latter kept going. Pritt dived again, this time opening fire. To his surprise, he saw one of the occupants begin to return fire with a pistol, so Pritt shot back with his Very pistol! The story was leaked to the press, and much to Pritt's embarrassment the following piece found its way into the newspapers, a copy of which was framed and hung on the No 66 Sqn Mess wall;

'The young knight of the air, drumming like a snipe and sweeping with hawk-like accuracy on his prey, but wishing to meet the German with his own weapons, shut off his machine gun and drew his revolver.'

Two of Pritt's squadron-mates claimed out-of-control victories over Albatros D IIIs on the 17th, and three days later Capt Taylor brought down a Rumpler C IV two-seater on the British side of the lines at 0910 hrs. The machine, which came from FA3, fell near Ypres, and it was re-designated G 63. The crew of Uffz Martin Ewald and Ltn Walter Rode were both killed.

Taylor and his flight had encountered two Rumplers, and they had stalked them for a while. However, when the Germans spotted their foes they quickly headed east. It was at this point that the Pup pilots attacked, Taylor exchanging fire with the rear gunner of one. Turning for another attack, he found the two-seater was nearly out of range, so he dived at the second. He opened fire from below, hammering rounds into its belly before the Pup stalled and spun away. Regaining control, Taylor watched as the Rumpler flew on, but now displaying a red glow which then turned into a smoke trail. Taylor was transfixed in shocked fascination as the Rumpler began to burn and the observer jumped into space, his arms and legs outstretched. The Rumpler finally crashed in flames near Brielen, its pilot probably already dead.

Pritt and Lascelles fought combats on the 21st, the former sending down a two-seater south-west of Roulers at 1145 hrs, while the latter forced a D III to land near the Ypres-Menin road that evening. Two No 54 Sqn aircraft were also shot up on this date, but both were repairable. The big news of the day for the Pups, however, was the destruction in flames of Zeppelin L23 off Lodbjerg, in Denmark.

The Pup had been carried aboard the cruiser HMS *Yarmouth*, which was engaged on a sweep off the Danish coast in company with the First Light Cruiser Squadron. At 0430 hrs, off Lyngvig, an airship was sighted, accompanied by a seaplane. It was felt that the airship was too near its home base to be intercepted, but it was hoped that by keeping it in sight it would continue its course away from Germany. About an hour later the airship was still in view and still heading north.

By now the fleet was off Lodbjerg Light, so a turn into wind was made and the ship launched Pup N6430, piloted by Sub-Lt B A Smart. Despite this being the first time he had flown off a ship, Smart left the platform without difficulty and climbed steadily to 7000 ft, setting course for the Zeppelin, which was now some 15 miles away. Smart climbed 1500 ft above the airship and attacked, firing 10 to 15 rounds from his wing-

mounted Lewis gun. His fire appeared to be too high, so he attacked again. This time he closed to within 20 yards of the stern before firing again. A sheet of flame shot out of the gas-bag and then the complete rear section seemed to be burning. The craft crumpled and plunged into the sea, taking Oblt z S Bernhard Dinter and his 18 crewmen to their deaths.

Heading back to the ships, Smart ditched close to HMS *Prince* and was rescued. Almost a year later, Capt Smart helped to destroy two more airships during a bombing raid on their sheds at Tondern. This time he was flying a Camel from HMS *Furious*.

Walmer-based Flt Cdr Kerby, who had shot down a Gotha bomber on 12 August, bagged another on the 22nd, this time off Margate, which together with Ramsgate and Dover had been targeted by a daylight raid of ten Gothas. A total of 138 home defence sorties was flown, and no less than three bombers were shot down. One fell on Hengrove golf course,

Pup N6443 was one of a handful of Scouts employed as ship-board fighters, being flown from several naval vessels. The fighter was launched from a platform mounted above one of the ship's gun turrets, the pilot then having to ditch alongside the vessel if he could not land ashore at the end of his sortie

Pup B5905 of No 61 Home Defence Squadron, based at Rochford, was lucky to survive this episode. The engine bearing sheared off in flight and two cylinders were lost, but the pilot made a successful controlled landing despite the dangling engine

L B Blaxland is seen seated in a No 61 Home Defence Squadron Pup in 1917. He had already scored at least two victories while flying Nieuport 17s and 23s with No 40 Sqn by the time he joined No 61 Sqn

Margate, another went down off Dover and the third went into the sea off Margate. All three came from, *Kampstaffel* 15, KG 3 and Kerby's was Gotha G IV 663. Ltns Werner Joschkowetz and Walter Latowski drowned, but gunner Uffz Bruno Schneider was plucked from the sea by sailors from HMS *Kestrel*.

During this attack, and unseen by Kerby, Canadian Flt Cdr G E Hervey, flying another Pup from Dover, had also attacked 663 and saw it start to go down. But other witnesses also saw Kerby's attack. Hervey's engine had oiled up as he followed the bomber down, and he had to make a forced landing on a nearby beach. For his part in the victory he received the DSC, while Kerby, who had received the DSC for his actions ten days earlier, failed to gain any further acknowledgment, despite his previous seven victories. More importantly, this was the last daylight bombing raid – after this the Gothas only came at night.

On 22 August, No 54 Sqn's 2Lt C G Wood claimed a black and white striped Albatros D V in flames over Middlekerke at 1900 hrs. Countering this success, a No 66 Sqn pilot became a PoW when his Pup came down east of Ostend due to engine failure. There was another loss for the squadron on the last day of August when a Pup crashed near Houthulst forest due to unknown circumstances.

No 46 Sqn welcomed new CO Maj S H Long DSO, MC in late August, although his tenure was to be a brief one for he took over after serving as a flight commander with No 24 Sqn. Soon tour-expired, he returned to

Capt H H deB Monk MC, AFC peers at the camera from the cockpit of a Pup at Gosport. Of interest is the cutaway engine cowling that also boasts two air intakes on the top. Monk won his MC with the King's Royal Rifle Corps before becoming a pilot

71

England having failed to add to his score of nine victories achieved with Nos 29 and 24 Sqns between August 1916 and March 1917.

LAST WEEKS AT THE FRONT

September saw the final Pup operations in France. Nos 46, 54 and 66 Sqns were now the only units flying the Sopwith Scout, with all the others having re-equipped with Camels.

Brewster-Joske of No 46 Sqn gained his fifth overall victory, and his fourth on Pups, by downing an Albatros scout near Menin at 1030 hrs on 3 September. Other than this one bright spot, the day was a disaster for the unit, as it lost four pilots in action during a bloody morning of combat. Three were taken prisoner, one died later of his wounds and the fourth was wounded while making a forced landing at No 23 Sqn's base. *Jasta* 11 and the leader of JG I accounted for two of them, Manfred von Richthofen scoring his 61st victory.

At 1135 hrs that same day, and in the same area, No 66 Sqn's Capt T V Hunter sent an Albatros scout down out of control for his fourth victory.

Early the following morning, 'Sticky' Hunter made his fifth claim when he got one of three Albatros scouts shot down out of control near Roulers by No 66 Sqn. The other two scorers were F A Smith and Pritt, the latter gaining his fifth victory too. It would appear that the fight was once again with *Jasta* 11, for the Pup pilots did not escape unscathed, losing Lt S A Harper MC to Ltn Eberhard Stapenhörst – it was the German's third victory. Oblt Willi Reinhard was wounded in the same action, the ace having scored six victories to date. He would go on to claim 20 and command JG I after von Richthofen was killed in April 1918.

No 66 Sqn also lost Capt C C Sharp in this battle, and like Harper, he too ended up a PoW. He had been downed by *Jasta* 11's Ltn Eberhardt Mohnicke for his seventh victory, the German ace having also claimed one of the No 46 Sqn Pups that had fallen the previous day.

Brewster-Joske made another claim on the 4th when he sent a D III down out of control east of Menin at 0800 hrs. Other squadron pilots then sent a two-seater down out of control at 0930 hrs south of the Scarpe. Those involved were Capt Scott, Lt Lee and 2Lts E Y Hughes, E Armitage, C W Odell and Court-neidge. This was Charles Walter Odell's first victory.

Born in Newport, on the Isle of Wight, in November 1898, Odell had initially served with the Inniskilling Fusiliers prior to joining the RFC. He would gain two victories on Pups and a further five on Camels by the autumn of 1918.

Squadron-mate, and fellow ace Eric Yorath Hughes was born in Brigend, South Wales, in July 1894. He scored four victories while flying

Capt Eric Hughes of No 46 Sqn claimed four of his five victories while flying Pups in 1917

Pups, and the fifth with a Camel. The Author interviewed him in 1968, when he recalled his first operational flight with No 46 Sqn after his arrival in June 1917;

'The morning after my arrival at No 46 Sqn, my flight commander, Cap (K W) McDonald asked how much flying I had done, and when I told him 18 hours in all, including dual at Netheravon, he said "My God, is that all? Well never mind, we are going on a line patrol and you just fly on my right. Stick by me, and if we run into any Huns don't turn and fire your gun, just turn and stay with me". Sure enough we did run into some Huns, and before I knew what was happening I was alone and rather frightened. I didn't know where I was or how to read a compass, but remembered to turn "where the golden sun sinks in the west" so I knew home was in the west, when suddenly I heard "ack-ack-ack-ack-ack".

'Turning my head round, I saw two Huns on my tail, both firing at me. I had never been so terrified in all my life. I remember murmuring, "Oh, God. Oh, Christ" repeatedly, putting my nose down with full engine and not having enough sense to even kick my rudder. I should have been cold meat, but for some unknown reason they left me and I eventually landed so far over our side of the lines that I must have been very near the English Channel. I expected a good ticking-off when I got back to the squadron, but got nothing of the sort, and was just told how lucky I had been, that I had to learn by experience and that it had been a lesson to me.'

Ken McDonald from County Kilkenny had been one of those lost to *Jasta* 11 on 3 September 1917, dying of wounds while in enemy hands the following day.

Later on the 4th, Arthur Lee shot down an Albatros scout at 1700 hrs. He recorded in his diary;

'I've got a Hun at last! And all on my own. And confirmed. An Albatros V-strutter, a D III. Coming back alone from a patrol, the formation split up and we made our separate ways. It was a lovely evening – very clear,

The Pup was also tested with Le Prieur rockets for anti-balloon attacks, this particular aircraft being photographed at Eastchurch during the trials

with a pale blue sky. I was gliding down just this side of the Hun balloon lines – for once "Archie" (AA fire) couldn't be bothered with just one aeroplane when I saw an RE 8 approaching on my left front, about 500 ft below. And tracers were spitting from the observer's gun. It was then that I realised that he was being followed and attacked by an Albatros V-strutter from about 150 yards range, also firing short bursts. Before I could react, the Hun ceased firing and turned east. I assumed he'd broken off because he'd spotted me. The RE 8 whizzed past below, the observer waved, and the Albatros continued on a level course eastwards.

'Suddenly I woke up and dropped into a wide sweeping curve that brought me dead behind the Hun, 200 ft above him. It seemed incredible that he hadn't seen me when he turned aside from the RE 8. It looked so easy I suspected a trap, and searched carefully around, but there was no other machine in sight. I came down closer and closer, holding my fire.

'My heart was pounding, and I was trembling uncontrollably, but my mind was calm and collected. I closed to ten yards, edged out of his slip-stream, drew nearer still until I saw that if I wasn't careful I'd hit his rudder. His machine was green and grey and looked very spick & span. He had a dark brown flying helmet, with a white goggle-strap round the back of his head. I aimed carefully through the Aldis between his shoulders just below where they showed above the fairing. It was impossible to miss. I gently pressed the trigger, and at the very first shots his head jerked back. Immediately the aeroplane reared up vertically. He must have clutched the joy-stick right back as he was hit. I followed upwards, still firing, until in two or three seconds he stalled and fell over to the left, and I had to slew sharply aside to avoid being hit. He didn't spin, but dropped into a near-vertical engine-on dive.'

Lee followed but the Albatros was going down so fast that he was unable to keep pace with it. It was still diving headlong when he heard gunfire close by, and two more D IIIs shot past him as he kicked his right rudder and skidded to one side. Lee was quick to slip back over the lines. Back home, he received confirmation of his victory from British AA gun positions that telephoned through to say that they had seen the Albatros disappear behind high ground where Lee was reporting it had gone down.

The day's other scorers were No 66 Sqn pilots Pritt and F A Smth, who each claimed Albatros scouts out of control over Roulers – this was Pritt's fifth victory. Reg Charley of No 54 Sqn claimed an Albatros scout on the 5th, which he saw fall into the sea off Slype at 1830 hrs. Earlier in the day, No 46 Sqn Pup pilots had encountered a single example of the new Fokker Dr I triplane fighter. There were only two at the front at this time, one being flown by von Richthofen and the other by Werner Voss, leader of *Jasta* 10. It was just before 1500 hrs (British time), and the patrol, made up of Capt Scott and Lts Hughes, Odell, Courtneidge and Armitage, was flying near Ypres. Their report stated;

'A formation of Sopwiths was approached by a triplane which was somewhat naturally thought to be English. It dived into the formation in company with an Albatros Scout. All pilots fired at it but it succeeded in getting away after being chased down to about 1000 ft.'

It was in fact Werner Voss in the Dr I, and his attack badly damaged the Pup (B1842) flown by Charlie Odell. The latter succeeded in coaxing his crippled fighter across the lines and down safely. German observers

No 46 Sqn's Pup A673 '5' was shot down by *Jasta* 12 on 16 September 1917. The machine had previously served with No 54 Sqn, where it had been used by Capt Oxspring and Lt F J Morse to score two victories apiece

reported that the Pup was irreparably damaged, thereby allowing Voss to claim his 40th victory. B1842 was, however, retrieved and sent to No 1 ASD for repair.

Despite the RNAS having all but stopped using its triplanes by this time, von Richthofen still managed to shoot down an RFC RE 8 on 1 September in his Dr I when the bomber's crew failed to spot that the three-winged machine closing on them was indeed an enemy aircraft.

The next Pup victories came on 11 September, when Capt Taylor of No 66 Sqn claimed an Albatros two-seater shot down trailing smoke near Eussen at 0800 hrs. Three hours later Scott, Lee, Hughes and Armitage sent an LVG two-seater down south of the Scarpe River, Capt Scott also claiming a scout out of control. Finally, Reg Charley of No 54 Sqn claimed a V-strutter out of control near Ostend at 1845 hrs to end a successful day for the Pup.

Patrick Taylor was almost at the end of his eight-month tour with No 66 Sqn, and he had been hoping to get some time in on the promised Camels, but it was not to be. He wrote;

'I knew that all the squadron could do was to hang on, survive somehow until it got a new type of aircraft. I lived from day to day with the hope that we might get the Camel. What a new world in the air that would open up if we were able to out-climb the Albatros! To have on the nose two Vickers guns, equal to the Hun's armament, and still be able to turn inside him, quicker even than the Pup!'

Brewster-Joske and 2Lt R N M Ferrie of No 46 Sqn each claimed Albatros scouts out of control in the early afternoon of the 16th, while 2Lt H H Maddocks of No 54 Sqn forced a D III to crash on fire east of Slype that same evening. His combat report records that;

'The enemy aircraft dived on 2Lt H H Maddocks' tail when he was attacking a two-seater. 2Lt. Maddocks did a climbing turn towards the enemy aircraft, who immediately pulled out of his dive. This gave 2Lt Maddocks a good position for a long burst at close range into the enemy aircraft, who turned and was fired at by most of the patrol. 2Lt Maddocks then got on the enemy aircraft's tail and got in a long burst, the enemy aircraft going down apparently on fire, and was followed down about 500 ft. This enemy aircraft was reported by No 48 Sqn to have gone down in flames and crashed.'

Five days were to pass before the next Pup victories, all of which fell to No 46 Sqn pilots. Scott, Odell, Hughes and Lee sent an LVG down out of control at 0820 hrs south of the Scarpe, but 2Lt R S Asher, although seen to force down an

No 46 Sqn's Lt R N M Ferrie runs up B1719 '4' at Filescamp Farm in September 1917. The mechanic leaning over the fighter's rear fuselage is endeavouring to keep the tail down while the pilot opens up the throttle

Albatros scout, was then himself shot down by Ulrich Neckel of *Jasta* 12. It was the German's first victory, and by war's end his score had reached 30 to gain him the *Pour le Mérite*. A short while later Odell and Lee were also engaged by Albatros scouts, and they were lucky to survive.

Once the fighting had ended, pilots claimed one Albatros destroyed (by 2Lt P W Wilcox) and two – possibly three – out of control by Capt V A H Robson, 2Lt P W S Bulman and Eric Hughes. Bulman would become a well-known test pilot for Hawkers after the war.

On the morning of the 22nd No 46 Sqn was again in the fighting, in company with four Bristol Fighters. Brewster-Joske and Ferrie destroyed an Albatros at 1010 hrs, while Capt Scott and Lee claimed two more out of control. This was all the work of 'C' Flight, which initially attacked a two-seater, Lee seemingly putting paid to the observer before the machine dived, well over the vertical. Shortly afterwards, five Albatros scouts came at them, and Lee once again found himself hard pressed. With tracer fire zipping past his nose, he nearly collided with another scout.

Lee eventually found himself upside down, looking right into the cockpit of the German machine, with its pilot looking up at him. For a moment Lee thought he was gazing into a mirror, for the enemy pilot's face looked just like his – not wearing goggles, and with an identical small moustache. The Albatros quickly disappeared from the scrap and Lee breathed a sigh of relief. He then spotted another D III closing in behind a Bristol Fighter. He attacked, and after firing 30 rounds saw the enemy machine jerk up, wing-over and fall away.

Two days later, on 24 September, 'C' Flight – Scott, Courtneidge, Armitage and Odell – sent a DFW two-seater down in flames over Havrincourt Wood at 1030 hrs. At 1240 hrs, Capt F J Morse and Hyde of No 54 Sqn claimed a brace of Albatros scouts.

Both squadrons gained victories on the 25th. At around 1130 hrs No 54 Sqn engaged several Albatros scouts 'up north', claiming three destroyed. Capt Oliver Stewart saw his crash into the sea off Middlekerke. Maddocks sent one down in flames in the same area, while the fire from M E Gonne's Pup caused his victim to break-up in the air and scatter itself over the sea. Only Ltn Johannes Wintrath from *Jasta* 2 'Boelcke' was killed during this engagement, and it is therefore possible that all three RFC pilots saw the same aircraft go in, which was not an uncommon occurrence.

Just before noon, Bulman, Wilcox and 2Lt G E Thomson of No 46 Sqn claimed a two-seater, which crashed near Pelves. This was George Thomson's first victory, and the only one he scored while flying a Pup – his next 20 would all be scored with a Camel, winning him the DSO and MC. He was killed in a flying accident in England in May 1918.

The Seaplane Defence Flight at Dunkirk was now using a mix of Camels and Pups, and the unit's last Pup combat came on the 29th when Leonard Slatter went up at night as raiders were bombing the area. This was a fairly regular occurrence, with so many airfields and depots in the Dunkirk area. In the gloom, he spotted a Gotha and attacked. Slatter watched it go down, obviously damaged, and it appeared to be heading for a forced-landing on the German side of the lines.

The last day of September saw Nos 46 and 66 Sqns share honours with two victories apiece. In the late morning, the latter unit had a scrap with some Albatros scouts, Capt T P H Bayetto claiming one, which crashed near Menin. Pritt got the other, this being his sixth and final victory in the Pup. He was flying B2162, which had a Lewis gun mounted on the top wing in addition to the Vickers. Awarded the MC, Pritt was subsequently rested – he later served with No 44 Home Defence Squadron.

However, neither of the men emerged from their combat on 30 September unscathed, for Bayetto was wounded and forced to make a landing near Kemmel, while Pritt also had to crash-land. In fact, the patrol, four Pups in total, had been in a fight with *Jasta* 18, with one pilot killed and another captured. *Jasta* 18 claimed four victories.

Capt Scott and Arthur Lee of No 46 Sqn were in action in the late afternoon of the 30th, Scott claiming two Albatros D Vs out of control near Vitry and Lee destroying a DFW two-seater. Scott, Lee, Odell and Armitage had found two DFWs well below them, Scott being on the verge of leading an attack when the Pups themselves were dived on by five Albatros scouts. They were instantly embroiled in a dogfight, Lee scrapping with a yellow and green scout that he appeared to hit several times, but as he later recalled, its pilot 'must have been wearing an iron suit', for the German seemed totally unhurt or unmoved.

Capt M D G 'Nobby' Scott MC and Capt C W Odell of No 46 Squadron both enjoyed success with the Pup in 1917. Scott achieved 11 of his 12 victories with the Pup, serving with both Nos 54 and 46 Sqns. Odell gained two of his seven claims with the Pup

Pup B6109 was photographed at an air depot in Egypt in August 1918, the veteran fighter having been fitted with a Lewis gun on its top wing

By this time the fight had attracted two Bristol Fighters and a DH 5, so the air was quite full of aeroplanes. Lee had one on his tail now, but 'Nobby' Scott managed to get it off. Then a Bristol flew right in front of Lee, who had to stall and spin away to avoid hitting it. In doing so he recovered near the two DFWs. Selecting the rearmost one, Lee attacked, receiving return fire from the gunner. After his initial pass, Lee went under the two-seater and zoomed up to fire into its belly. The DFW reared up, went over sideways onto its back and dived. Lee watched it fall a long way, and one of the Bristol crews later confirmed it had gone in.

Meanwhile, more fighting with the Albatros scouts resulted in Scott sending down his second, although Armitage was wounded in the leg but managed to get home. He seemed to be all right and cheerful about his 'Blighty' wound, but on 4 October he died of gangrene poisoning.

The DFW was Lee's fifth victory, while the Albatros scouts were Scott's 11th and 12th (and last) claims. The latter also received the MC, and he too was sent home in early October, only to be killed in a flying accident at Shoreham on 17 March 1918 while serving with No 91 Sqn.

Lee and Brewster-Joske shared an Albatros D V on 11 October during a large combined offensive patrol in company with Bristol Fighters of No 11 Sqn and DH 5s of No 41 Sqn. Brewster-Joske led the whole show. One Pup dived too steeply, got into the midst of the enemy machines from *Jasta* 12 and was shot down. Ltn Walter Ewers claimed the downed Pup for his third of eight victories. Lee and Brewster-Joske hammered another Albatros and sent it spinning down with pieces falling from it.

Two days later No 54 Sqn was bounced from above whilst on patrol and four Pups were lost. Two pilots were killed and two captured. The unit experienced better luck on 18 October, however, with aces Hyde and Gonne destroying a D V near Pervyse at 1430 hrs. This was George Hyde's fifth, and last victory, and Michael Gonne's second. Londoner Gonne would gain three more on Camels, winning him the MC. After taking leave, which began in March 1918, he returned to No 54 Sqn on 7 August 1918, only to be killed in action the very next day.

Pup B1812 of No 61 Home Defence Squadron has its Vickers gun tested in the butts at Rochford in the summer of 1917. This aircraft was regularly flown by Lionel Blaxland

Pups serving in England on home defence and training duties often took on a very different appearance to those in France. Here, B2192 has been painted with broad black and white stripes during its time with the School of Special Flying at Gosport in the summer of 1917. Future nine-victory Camel ace Capt H H Balfour MC and Capt E L Foot MC both flew this machine while serving with the school

The Pup's days in France were now numbered, as Camels were starting to replace them in Nos 46, 54 and 66 Sqns. The October weather was also starting to restrict flying. Everyone was hoping it would not be too long before the new Camels totally re-equipped their units, and No 46 Sqn received its first examples on 7 November.

Eleven days prior to this, on 28 October, the unit's Ferrie and 2Lt J H Cooper sent an Albatros scout down out of control, although Cooper had to make a forced landing. His Pup was wrecked, but he escaped injury. Maddocks and 2Lt S J Schooley of No 54 Sqn sent a DIII down north of Dixmude on 4 November, while on the 12th, Charley and Hyde – now a captain – claimed a scout and a DFW out of control respectively.

The honour of claiming the very last Pup victory went to future ace Eric Hughes of No 46 Sqn. He destroyed an Albatros scout south of Cambrai at 0910 hrs on 1 December. The only German loss recorded was that of Ltn Walter Brashcwitz of *Jasta* 17, who came down near Marcoing. Badly wounded, he died in hospital on the 23rd. It was Hughes' fourth victory, and by the time he scored his fifth later in the month he was a flight commander with No 3 Sqn, flying Camels.

By the end of 1917 the Pup had passed into history. Some were still employed on Home Defence duties in England, and in numerous training schools and squadrons. It was still a very nice aeroplane to fly, with virtually no vices. And it is likely that coming from the docile Pup, the Camel was something of a shock to a new pilot's system. The Camel was not a forgiving aircraft, and many young men were killed during their early flights. Camels were vicious in a loop unless actually 'flown' through the manoeuvre. Trying to loop a Camel like a Pup by just pulling back on the stick and letting it go over was invariably fatal. But that story has already been told in Osprey's *Aircraft of the Aces 52 - Sopwith Camel Aces of World War 1*.

APPENDICES

Notes on Aerial Fighting in Formation by Flt Lt C R Mackenzie of 8 Naval Squadron

Type of Machine considered – 80 hp Le Rhone Sopwith Scout (Pup)
Number of Machines – five

The Flight Leader

In the first place, he must choose suitable pilots to fly together, and having chosen them, must let them always fly together, and in the same positions in the formation, as far as possible. He must endeavour never to let a pilot fly any machine but his own over the lines.

He is responsible for his flight leaving the ground punctually and, to make certain of this, must ensure that all pilots are dressed and comfortably settled in their machines five minutes before the flight is due to start.

All engines having been previously run by the petty officer, must be seen to be ticking over. Then, on a signal from the petty officer that all engines are satisfactory, the flight leaves the ground in 30 seconds, the order of getting off corresponding to each machine's position in the formation, thus;

```
              1
          2       3
        4           5
```

The leader must fly full-out to about 700 ft and in an absolutely straight direction. He then throttles right down and flies his machine as slowly as possible, in the meantime watching his pilots pick up the formation (this should not take more than one or two minutes). This done, he gives the 'attention' signal by rocking his machine laterally, or by firing a red Very light, turns and heads to the lines, or as he thinks fit, and opens up his engine when the turn is absolutely completed. The formation then begins to climb, and the leader must adjust his engine to the worst climbing machine as quickly as possible and, having done that, alter his throttle speed and direction as little as possible. He must look round at his formation at least every minute. Do not use a too tight a V-formation, as this leaves three rear machines open to attack instead of two.

The Flying Officer

It is of paramount importance for a flying officer to be able to use his throttle to the full, and to be thoroughly able to alter the angle of climb of his machine. This sounds extraordinarily easy, but it is the root of the trouble of all bad formation pilots. They will not use their throttle and alter the speed of their machine.

Having left the ground, each pilot picks up his allotted station in order – i.e. as close as possible and slightly above his next ahead – and throttles right down. When flying in formation, pilots should fly as close as possible

together, and the angle subtended by the formation must not be acute, otherwise the leader cannot see his machines if they get too far behind him without turning his head excessively.

There is no excuse for a pilot being astern of station, and if he is above his next ahead, he must put his nose down and catch up. Having once picked up formation, it leads to endless trouble if a flying officer loses position and starts doing circles on his own. The slightest mistakes in position must be instantly corrected – do not wait until the error is a big one. An exact parallel is found in steering a boat or a car. A good helmsman keeps on his course by employing none but the smallest motions of the tiller. The evolution of altering course is more difficult. The flight leaders should always endeavour to turn to the same direction, assuming this to be left, thus giving each pilot a chance to learn his own particular job.

The flight leader rocks his machine repeatedly and pauses and then he does a minute turn to the left, at the same time throttling down and putting his nose down a little. The two pilots on his left do a slight right hand turn, throttling down a little more. The two pilots on his right commence a left hand turn, keeping their engines full out. Then the pilots on his left both do a steep left hand turn, the leader turns to the left and the two right hand pilots carry on with their left hand turn. Then the leader straightens out and the formation picks up its dressing and the leader opens his engine and carries on as before. This is by far the most successful method of turning a formation.

No further point should present great difficulty on this side of the lines. Pilots must remember to fire their guns as continuously as possible to prevent freezing, keeping in mind the bullet's destination. Also remember to look behind and towards your formation, thus helping to prevent a surprise attack on the other formation 'arms'.

On Crossing the Lines

In enemy territory, Hostile Aircraft and anti-aircraft fire make an accurate formation a matter of some difficulty, and in practice machines fly more in a group than in a formation, but the more accurate the formation the easier is the task for the already overworked leader. The leader has to keep his formation together, to decide when to attack hostile aircraft, to watch for Hostile Aircraft about to attack, to see his formation does not lose its way and to attend to many other small points. The flying officer's main duty is to keep formation on the leader and watch out for being attacked. The latter applies most to the two rear pilots.

Signals between Machines

These are in practice mostly given by the leader: (a) rocking the machine laterally to call attention to anything, and if accompanied by waving the arm, it calls attention to hostile aircraft in that direction. If followed by rocking the machine in a fore/aft direction, it means a gun jam; (b) a green light means an escort to the lines for engine failure or any other reason.

Never wave except to indicate Hostile Aircraft

If a pilot wishes to communicate with the leader he must get in front of him and give the signal. If unable to do this he must communicate somehow with another pilot and he will warn the leader. The leader must on no account allow a returning pilot to cross the lines unescorted.

Do not continually call the leader's attention to Hostile Aircraft, as he has probably already seen them, and has good reason for not attacking. If a machine gets out of touch with the formation, he must go to a previously arranged spot for reforming.

Attacking Hostile Aircraft

The following ten commandments in aerial fighting are considered of vital importance. They may appear cowardly, but they are compiled from the experience of the pilots of this squadron, as well as many experienced RFC pilots. The man who gets the most Huns in his lifetime is the man who observes these commandments and fights with his head. The others either get killed or get nerves in a very short time, and the country does not get the full benefit of having trained them.

1. Do not lose formation.
2. Do not press an attack on a two-seater who fires at you before you are in perfect position. Break away and attack him or another Hostile Aircraft later with a chance of surprise.
3. Do not stay to manoeuvre with a two-seater.
4. Do not dive to break off combat. German machines are the better divers but worse climbers than our machines as a rule.
5. Do not unnecessarily attack a superior formation – you will get a better chance if you wait five minutes.
6. Do not attack without looking for the machine above you – he will most certainly come onto your tail unawares while you are attacking if you are not watching him. Look behind continually on a dive.
7. Do not come down too low on the other side or you will have all the Huns in Christendom on you.
8. Do not go to sleep in the air for one instant of your patrol. Watch your tail.
9. Do not deliver a surprise attack at over 90 knots unless you wish to scare Hostile Aircraft off a friendly machine's tail. Most machines are not easily controlled at that speed and the firing period passes too rapidly.
10. Do not deliver a surprise attack at over 100 yards range at the very most.

Delivering an Attack

In delivering an attack, remember that your most important asset is surprise. The commonest ways to effect this are: 1) wait until the enemy machine is going away from the sun and come in on his tail; 2) dive from a big height; 3) if you have a marked ascendancy in climb, come in from below and behind (this method has its obvious drawbacks); and 4) attack while he is obviously otherwise engaged. Thus, it is often not wise to immediately attack sometimes. It pays, too, to find out what is the object of the enemy's flight and attack him whilst carrying out this object, and least likely to be on the lookout – e.g. photography. While he is attacking or waiting to attack a machine, an enemy presents little or no defensive fire. When shadowing Hostile Aircraft, keep as far away as possible, and keep sunwards of him. Do not forget that a single enemy machine at low altitude is probably bait and a counter-attack must be anticipated.

With regard to the method of attack, it is usually best and easiest to attack from behind. These eight angle attacks through the wing are not usually successful. Attacking from in front is not to be recommended. In practice, the method of attacking from behind is the most used. But it is very easy to make a mess of an easy chance. Try and discover if you have the speed of the Hostile Aircraft flying level (always assuming you are above him). If you have not, glide straight down to him and attack on the steep glide, withholding fire until very close – i.e. 100 yards. If you *have*, dive well behind him and come up to him very slightly lower on the throttle. If the attack is a surprise, place yourself about 25 yards behind him, very slightly below, and throttle down to his exact speed, then fire. You want to have a hand on the throttle at all times, and of course the joystick trigger should always be on.

This method of attack seems very simple, but as in all things, the more practice the better. It is very easy to lose speed too far astern and be so long in catching up that you are observed, or to have too much speed and shoot by the enemy machine. The most difficult part of all is to withhold fire till the correct moment. Pilots learn their own methods of attack from experience, but this will be found a good one to try, especially in a Sopwith 80 hp Le Rhône Scout. If, before you are in a position to fire, you see the observer produce his gun, make off at once. Do not stay to scrap and manoeuvre with the two-seater. A scout is designed for offensive and has absolutely no defensive, except its performance.

When the leader attacks, it is usual for two and three to accompany him down. Two is supposed to attack the same machine as the leader, but in practice things arrange themselves. If two machines manage to attack an enemy simultaneously, it more than doubles the chance of success. Four and five remain aloft for a short period to guard the tails of one, two and three, and then join in if one, two and three are not attacked. It will be readily understood that in the case of one formation attacking another, no rules of combat can be laid down.

A very pleasant help in time of trouble is to put yourself in the enemy's place and view the situation from his point of view. If you feel frightened before an attack, just think how frightened he must be.

On being Attacked

The German will not often attack unless at a very great advantage. If you see a hostile machine above you, try and climb above him. If this fails, try and get into his blind spot below the lower plane and then turn and try to lose him. You can always shake him off by going back to the lines, or joining a friendly formation. If you are already in a formation, he will probably not attack. If you see that he has got to attack, steer a straight course for the lines, unless that course is away from the sun, and wait for him to dive. Do not turn or twist the moment he starts to dive or he will stop and you will have to go through it again. Wait until he is nearly within decisive range, then put

your nose down slightly and do a turn – that is quite sufficient to make him miss, and he will probably carry on his dive. If you suddenly hear a machine fire on your tail, do a side loop at once. In all fighting in the air, keep your head, put yourself in the enemy's position and don't unnecessarily tackle any chance less that an even one.

Author's note – Flt Lt C R Mackenzie was killed in action in a Pup on 24 January 1917

PUP ACES

Name	Squadron/s	Claims on Type	War Total
Flt Cdr J S T Fall	3N	11	36
Capt M D G Scott	54/46	11	12
Flt Sub-Lt J J Malone	3N	10	10
Flt Cdr F D Casey	3N	9	9
Flt Lt H S Kerby	9N/3N/Walmer Def Flt	9	9
Capt C A Brewster-Joske	46	8	9
Flt Sub-Lt L F W Smith	4N	8	8
Capt O M Sutton	54	8	9
Flt Cdr L S Breadner	3N	7	10
Maj S J Goble	8N	6	10
Capt F N Hudson	54	6	6
Flt Lt E Pierce	3N/9N	6	9
Lt W A Pritt	66	6	6
Capt J O Andrews	66	5	12
Flt Cdr F C Armstrong	3N	5	13
Flt Lt A W Carter	3N	5	17
Flt Cdr A J Chadwick	4N	5	11
Capt R M Charley	54	5	5
Flt Lt J A Glen	3N	5	15
Flt Lt E R Grange	1W/8N	5	5
Capt T V Hunter	66	5	6
Capt G A Hyde	54	5	5
Capt A S G Lee	46	5	7
Capt S H Pratt	46	5	7
Capt O M Stewart	54	5	5
Capt W V Strugnell	54	5	6
Capt P G Taylor	66	5	5
Flt Cdr H G Travers	3N	5	5
Flt Cdr A T Whealy	3N	5	27

ACES WHO SCORED VICTORIES FLYING THE PUP

Name	Squadron/s	Claims on Type	War Total
Flt Sub-Lt A J Enstone	4N	4	13
Flt Lt D M B Galbraith	8N	4	6
Capt E Y Hughes	46	4	5
Capt T V Hunter	66	4	5
Capt T C Luke	66	4	6
Capt H H Maddocks	54	4	7
Flt Sub-Lt G W Hemming	4N	3	6
Capt R A Little	8N	3	47
Capt L H Rochford	3N	3	29
Flt Cdr A M Shook	4N	3	12
Flt Cdr F E Banbury	9N	2	10
Flt Sub-Lt S E Ellis	4N	2	5
Capt M E Gonne	54	2	5
Capt C W Odell	46	2	7
Capt R R Soar	8N	2	12
Maj C D Booker	8N	1	29
Capt A R Brown	11N	1	10
Lt R M Foster	54	1	16
Maj R Graham	SDF	1	5
Capt N Keeble	1W	1	6
Capt M C McGregor	54	1	11
Capt L H Slatter	SDF	1	7
Flt Sub-Lt H F Stackard	9N	1	15
Capt G E Thomson	46	1	21

BREAKDOWN OF INDIVIDUAL PUP ACES' SCORES

	Enemy Aircraft Type	Claim	Location	Time	Pup
Joe Fall					
1917					
6 April	Halberstadt D II	crashed	Bourlon Wood	1020	A6158
11 April	Albatros D II	ooc	Cambrai	0900	A6158
"	Albatros D II	crashed	Cambrai	0905	A6158
"	Albatros D II	ooc	Cambrai	0905	A6158
23 April	Albatros D III	crashed	Bourlon Wood	1730	N6205
29 April	Albatros D III	ooc	Bois de Grand	1100	N6205
1 May	Albatros D III	ooc	Epinoy	1045	N6205
23 May	Albatros D III	ooc	W Bourlon	1345	N6479
7 July	seaplane	crashed	N Ostend	1110	N6479
"	seaplane	crashed	NW Ostend	1115	N6479
"	Albatros D V	flames	Ostend	1220	N6479

25 victories flying Camels

Maurice Scott

1916
First victory flying a Vickers FB 5 with No 18 Sqn

1917

5 April	balloon	destroyed	Gouy	?	A636
9 May	two-seater	crashed	Seranvillers	1530	A7330
11 May	two-seater	crashed	Walincourt	1840	A6165
1 June	Albatros D III	ooc	Honnecourt	1135	A7330
4 September	Albatros C	ooc	S Scarpe	0930	B1843
11 September	two-seater	ooc	S Scarpe	1055	B2191
21 September	two-seater	ooc	S Scarpe	0820	B2191
22 September	Albatros D V	ooc	Sailly en Ostrevent	01030	B2191
24 September	DFW C	crashed	SE Honnecourt	1030	B2191
30 September	Albatros D V	ooc	Vitry	1630	B2191
"	Albatros D V	ooc	Vitry	1636	B2191

John Malone

1917

4 March	Halberstadt D II	ooc	Manancourt	1145	9898
17 March	two-seater	ooc	NE Bapaume	1025	9898
"	Albatros D II	flames	Ervillers	1100	9898
"	Albatros D II	flames	Arras	1450	9898
21 April	two-seater	ooc	N Queant	1740	N6208
23 April	Albatros D III	crashed	Croiselles	0630	N6208
"	Albatros D III	ooc	Croiselles	0715	N6208
"	Albatros D III	ooc	Croiselles	0745	N6208
24 April	DFW C	captured	Morchies	1650	N6208
26 April	Albatros D III	crashed	N Cambrai	1915	N6202

Francis Casey

1917

17 March	Halberstadt D II	ooc	NE Bapaume	1040	N6163
8 April	Albatros D III	ooc	NE Pronville	1500	N6182
21 April	Albatros D III	crashed	Hendecourt	1730	N6182
"	Albatros D III	ooc	Hendecourt	1730	N6182
23 April	Albatros D III	ooc	Cagnicourt	1730	N6182
24 April	DFW C	captured	Morchies	1650	N6182
26 April	Albatros D III	ooc	Cambrai	1915	N6182
29 April	Albatros D III	flames	Cambrai	1100	N6182
2 May	Albatros D III	ooc	Moevres	1120	N6182

Harold Kerby

1917

24 March	seaplane	crashed	Wenduyne	1100	N6177
22 April	Albatros C	ooc	Cambrai	1910	N6160
23 April	Albatros D III	crashed	Le Pave	1730	N6160
"	Albatros D III	crashed	Le Pave	1730	N6160
6 May	Albatros D III	ooc	Bourlon Wood	1905	N6465
"	Albatros D III	ooc	Lagnicourt	1905	N6465
27 May	Albatros D III	crashed	Villers	0745	N6465
12 August	Gotha G IV	crashed	off Southend	2000	N6440
22 August	Gotha G IV	crashed	off Margate	1045	N6440

Clive Brewster-Joske

1916
First victory flying Morane Parasol with No 1 Sqn

1917

2 June	Albatros D III	ooc	Houthulst	1800	B1709
3 June	Albatros D III	crashed	?	?	A7335
7 June	Albatros D III	crashed	Wervicq-Comines	1030	B1709
17 June	Albatros D V	ooc	Lens	1930	B1709
3 September	Albatros D V	crashed	Menin	1030	B1709
4 September	Albatros D V	ooc	E Menin	0800	A7335
16 September	Albatros D III	ooc	Ecoust St Quentin	1315	A7335
22 September	Albatros D III	crashed	N Brebieres	1015	A7335
11 October	Albatros D V	ooc?	L Marquion	1645	A7335

Langley Smith

1917

30 April	Albatros D II	ooc	E Nieuport	1245	N6168
9 May	balloon	destroyed	Ghistelles	0800	N6168
"	two-seater	crashed	SE Ghistlles	1715	N6168
12 May	Albatros D III	crashed	off Zeebrugge	0730	N6168
25 May	Gotha G	crashed	N Westende	1830	N6168
5 June	balloon	destroyed	Ostend	0440	N6168
6 June	Albatros D V	crashed	N Handzaeme	1520	N6168
"	Albatros D V	ooc	N Handzaeme	1520	N6168

Lloyd Breadner

1917

6 April	Halberstadt D II	crashed	Bourlon Wood	1020	N5199
11 April	Albatros C	flames	Cambrai	0845	N6181
"	Albatros D III	crashed	Cambrai	0855	N6181
23 April	Gotha G II	captured	Vron	1030	N6181
"	Albatros D III	ooc	Bourlon Wood	1730	N6181
29 April	Albatros D III	ooc	SE Cambrai	1115	N6181
23 May	Albatros D III	ooc	Awoingt-Cambrai	1345	N6197

Three victories flying Camels

Oliver Sutton

1917

2 April	two-seater	ooc	E Péronne	0800	A637
11 May	two-seater	crashed	Walincourt	1840	A6183
24 May	Albatros D III	crashed	Prémont	0810	A6183
1 June	Albatros D III	crashed	Gonnelieu	1125	A6183
"	Albatros D III	ooc	Honnecourt	1130	A6183
3 June	Albatros D III	ooc	Gouy	0645	A6183
5 June	Albatros D III	ooc	Brebieres	0700	A6183
6 June	Albatros D III	crashed	SW Cambrai	1200	A6183

One victory flying a Camel

Stan Goble

1916
Two victories flying Nieuports with 1 Naval Wing, and his first Pup victory was also scored whilst with this Wing prior to moving to 8 Naval Squadron

1916

22 September	LVG C	ooc	Ghistelles	1530	3691
16 November	LVG C	ooc	Gommecourt	1055	N5194
17 November	two-seater	crashed	Bapaume	1535	N5194
27 November	two-seater	flames	SE Bapaume	0950	N5194
4 December	Halberstadt D II	ooc	SE Bapaume	1100	N5194
11 December	two-seater	ooc	E Bucquoy	1010	N5194

Two victories flying with 'Naval 5' in 1918

Frank Hudson

1917

27 January	two-seater	flames	Courcelette	1410	A652
13 February	two-seater	ooc	Le Transloy	1045	A652
5 April	balloon	destroyed	Gouy	?	A6166
6 April	two-seater	ooc	Le Catelet	0730	A6166
26 April	Albatros D III	ooc	Prémont	1910	A6166
11 July	Albatros C	crashed	NE Nieuport	0410	A6246

Ed Pierce

1917

12 April	Albatros D II	ooc	Pronville	1030	N6171
"	Albatros D II	ooc	Pronville	1030	N6171
22 April	Albatros D III	ooc	Cambrai	1915	N6171
23 April	Albatros D III	ooc	Croiselles	0630	N6171
2 May	Albatros C	flames	Bourlon Wood	0700	N6171
11 May	two-seater	crashed	Noordschoote	1200	9928

Three victories flying Sopwith Triplanes and Camels

Walbanke Pritt

1917

28 July	Albatros D III	crashed	E Roulers	1930	B1762
16 August	Albatros D V	crashed	Marcke	0515	B1732
"	Albatros D V	crashed	Marcke	0515	B1732
21 August	Aviatik C	crashed	SW Roulers	1145	B1762
4 September	Albatros D III	ooc	Roulers	0715	B2162
30 September	Albatros D V	crashed	?	1115	B2162

John Andrews

1916

Seven victories flying DH 2s with No 24 Sqn

1917

30 April	Albatros C	crashed	Brebieres	0845	A6177
2 May	Albatros D II	crashed	Orchies	1415	A6177
13 May	Albatros D III	ooc	?	0800	B1703
7 June	two-seater	crashed	Gheluvelt	0800	B1703
11 July	Albatros C	crashed	Henin-Lietard	1035	B1703

Fred Armstrong

1917

6 April	Halberstadt D II	ooc	Bourlon Wood	1020	N6178
12 April	Albatros D II	ooc	Pronville	1030	N6178
2 May	Albatros C	Flames	Bourlon Wood	0700	N6178
6 May	Albatros D III	ooc	Bourlon Wood	1905	N6178
7 July	seaplane	crashed	N Ostend	1110	N6465

Eight victories flying Camels

Alfred Carter

1917

6 April	Halberstadt D III	ooc	Bourlon Wood	1020	N6160
23 April	Albatros D III	crashed	Epinoy	1730	N6179
"	Albatros D III	ooc	Epinoy	1800	N6179
29 April	Albatros D III	ooc	SE Cambrai	1115	N6179
27 May	Albatros D III	ooc	E Bullencourt	0740	N6474

12 victories flying Camels

Arnold Chadwick

1917

26 April	Albatros D II	ooc	Steenbrugh	1530	N9899
25 May	Albatros C	crashed	off Bray Dunes	0535	N6176
"	Gotha G	crashed	N Westende	1830	N6176
26 May	two-seater	crashed	SW Furnes	0845	N6176
3 June	Albatros D V	crashed	Cortemarck	1640	N6176

Six victories flying Camels

Reg Charley

1917

26 April	Albatros D III	ooc	Prémont	1910	A672
13 July	Albatros D III	ooc	N of Yser	1315	A672
5 September	Albatros D V	crashed	off Slype	1830	A6203
11 September	Albatros D V	ooc	nr Ostend	1845	A7344
12 November	Albatros D V	ooc	nr Westende	1345	A6203

Jimmy Glen

1917

23 May	Albatros D III	ooc	Bourlon Wood	1340	N6183
27 May	Albatros D III	crashed	Ecoust St Quentin	0730	N6183
17 June	DFW C	ooc	NE Ypres	0630	N6479
7 July	seaplane	crashed	N Ostend	1110	N6183
"	seaplane	crashed	NW Ostend	1120	N6183

Ten victories flying Camels

Edward Grange

1916

25 September	seaplane	crashed	off Ostend	1200	N5182

1917

4 January	Albatros D II	crashed	N Bapaume	1500	N5194
"	Albatros D II	ooc	N Bapaume	1500	N5194
"	Albatros D II	ooc	N Bapaume	1500	N5194
7 January	Albatros D II	ooc	Grevillers	1100	N5194

Tom Hunter

1917

12 July	Albatros D III	ooc	NE Ypres	2000	B1760
27 July	Albatros D III	crashed	Ardoye	1700	B1760
28 July	Albatros D III	ooc	E Roulers	2100	B1760
3 September	Albatros D V	ooc	NE Menin	1135	B1760
4 September	Albatros D V	ooc	Roulers	0715	B1760

One victory flying a Camel

George Hyde

1917

17 March	two-seater	ooc	E Roye	1135	A649
30 April	Albatros D III	ooc	Walincourt	0630	A649
12 August	Albatros D III	ooc	?	?	B1792
24 September	Albatros D V	ooc	Mannekensvere	1240	A6156
18 October	Albatros D V	crashed	Leke	1430	B1792

Arthur Lee

1917

4 September	Albatros D V	ooc	NE Polygon Wood	1700	B1777
11 September	LVG	ooc	S Scarpe River	1055	B1777
21 September	LVG C	ooc	S Scarpe River	0820	B1777
22 September	Albatros D V	ooc	Sailly en Ostrevent	1030	B1777
30 September	DFW C	ooc	Vitry	1635	B1777

Two victories flying Camels

Stuart Pratt

1917

Pratt claimed two victories with Nieuport 12s flying with No 46 Sqn

25 May	Albatros D	ooc	?	?	A7327
3 June	Albatros D	ooc	?	?	A7327
5 June	Albatros D III	ooc	?	?	A7327
15 June	DFW C	ooc	Ploegsteert	1050	A7327
17 June	Albatros D V	ooc	Lens	1930	A7327

Oliver Stewart

1917

6 April	Albatros D III	crashed	St Quentin	0800	A6156
24 May	Albatros D III	ooc	Prémont	0800	A6156
6 June	Albatros D III	crashed	SW Cambrai	1200	A6156
15 August	two-seater	crashed	S Middlekerke	0730	A6211
25 September	Albatros D V	crashed	N Middlekerke	1130	A6211

William Strugnell

1916

One victory with No 1 Sqn flying a Morane P

1917

19 March	two-seater	flames	Roisel	0745	?
14 April	two-seater	ooc	Buissy-Inchy	0815	A7306
1 May	Albatros D III	ooc	E St Quentin	0710	A7306
11 May	two-seater	crashed	Walincourt	1840	A6168
"	Albatros D III	crashed	Beaurevoir	1910	A6168

Patrick Gordon Taylor

1917

7 May	Albatros D III	FTL	S Oppy	?	A7309
7 June	Albatros C	ooc	Gheluvelt	0800	A7309
15 June	Albatros C	ooc	N Passchendaele	0820	A7309
20 August	Albatros C	captured	NW Ypres	0910	B1757
11 September	Albatros C	ooc	Eussen	0800	B1757

Herbert Travers

1917

11 March	Albatros C	ooc	Bapaume	1150	N6175
17 March	Albatros D III	ooc	Pronville	1050	N6175
8 April	Albatros D III	ooc	NE Pronville	1510	N6169
21 April	Albatros D III	ooc	Cagnicourt	1730	N6169
24 April	DFW C	captured	Morchies	1650	N6169

Art Whealy

1917

12 April	Albatros D III	ooc	Pronville	1030	N6194
23 April	Albatros D III	ooc	Arras-Cambrai Rd	1800	N6194
2 May	Albatros C	flames	Bourlon Wood	0700	N6194
9 May	Halberstadt D II	ooc	?	1230	N6167
7 July	Albatros D V	ooc	SW Haynecourt	1730	N6174

22 victories flying Triplanes and Camels

SUCCESSFUL PUP AIRFRAMES (five or more kills)

Number	Victories	Squadron/s	Aces	Markings
9899	5	4N	Chadwick, Enstone, Hemming	*DO-DO*
N5194	8	8N	Goble, Grange, Little	-
N5196	7	8N/4N	Galbraith, Goble	'T' (8N)
N6160	6	3N	Collishaw, Carter, Kerby	-
N6168	8	4N	Smith	-
N6169	9	3N	Travers	-
N6171	5	3N	Pierce	'P'/*BLACK ARROW*
N6178	5	3N	Armstrong	-
N6179	6	3N/SDF	Carter, Slatter	*BABY MINE*
N6181	5	3N	Breadner	*HMA HAPPY*
N6182	8	3N	Casey	-
N6208	5	3N	Malone	-
N6479	5	3N	Fall, Glen	-
A6156	5	54	Stewart	'OS' monogram
A6168	6	54	Cole, Strugnell	-
A6183	7	54	Sutton	-
A7306	5	54	Strugnell	-
A7327	5	46	Pratt	1/skull & crossbone
A7330	5	54/46	Scott	-
A7335	5	46	Brewster-Joske	-
B1703	5	66	Andrews	'I'
B1760	5	66	Hunter	-
B1777	7	46	Lee	*CHIN-CHOW*/'4'
B2191	7	46	Scott	-

OPERATIONAL PUP SQUADRONS IN FRANCE

Unit	Bases	Commanding Officers
No 46 Sqn RFC	Boisdinghem La Gorgue Bruay Suttons Farm St-Marie-Cappel Izel-le-Hameau	Maj P Babington
No 54 Sqn RFC	St Omer Chipilly Flez Bray Dunes Leffrinckhoucke	Maj K K Horn
No 66 Sqn RFC	St Omer Vert Galand Liettres Calais Hornchurch Estrée-Blanche	Maj O T Boyd Maj G L P Henderson
3 Naval Squadron RNAS	Vert Galand Bertangles Marieux Furnes	Sqn Cdr R H Mulock
4 Naval Squadron RNAS	Coudekirke Bray Dunes	Sqn Cdr B L Huskisson
8 Naval Squadron RNAS	St Pol Vert Galand	Sqn Cdr G R Bromet
9 Naval Squadron RNAS	St Pol Furnes	Sqn Cdr H Fawcett
Seaplane Defence Flight	Dunkirk	Sqn Cdr R Graham

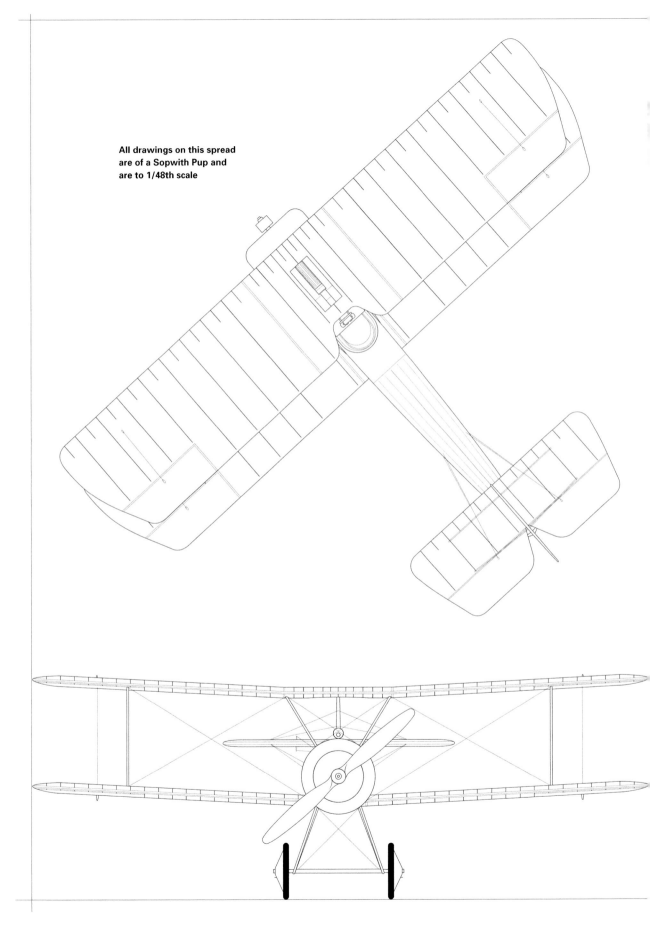

All drawings on this spread
are of a Sopwith Pup and
are to 1/48th scale

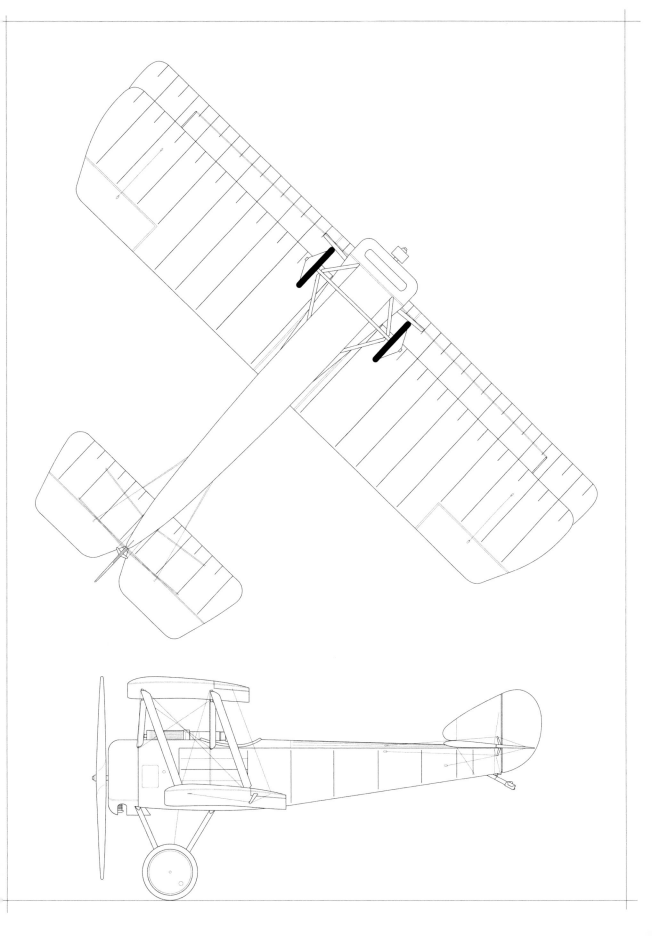

1

Pup N6171 of Flt Sub-Lt E Pierce, 3 Naval Squadron, Marieux, France, April 1917

This 'C' Flight machine was usually flown by Flt Sub-Lt Edmund Pierce in March 1917. It is coded 'P', and beneath the cockpit rim displays the name *BLACK ARROW*, below which is a white-outlined black arrow motif. The front section of the Pup's cowling is also painted black to identify its flight assignment. Pierce claimed two victories on 12 April, but on the 14th the machine blew over in high winds at Marieux, although it was only slightly damaged. In all, Pierce had scored five victories in N6171 by 6 May, when the fighter was damaged in a landing accident with new pilot Oliver LeBoutillier (a future ten-victory ace) at the controls. Repaired once again, N6171 later served with the Seaplane Defence Flight at Dunkirk, before finally ending its days with the newly formed Royal Air Force as an instructional airframe at the RAF College at Cranwell.

2

Pup N6181 of Flt Cdr L S Breadner, 3 Naval Squadron, Marieux, France, April 1917

Canadian Lloyd Breadner flew this machine during 'Bloody April' 1917, scoring five victories with it during the course of the month. As with many RNAS aircraft of World War 1, it displays a name below the cockpit. These typically referred to the wives or girlfriends of the pilot assigned to the aircraft, but in N6181's case, it seems to have reflected Breadner's demeanour! Just above the 'H' are the the small white letters *HMA*, which possibly stands for His Majesty's Aircraft. The Pup displays 'Naval 3's' identification stripe along the fuselage, which was repeated on the top fuselage decking and across the top wing centre section. The front part of the Pup's cowling has been painted red, which was 'B' Flight's assigned colour.

3

Pup N6205 of Flt Cdr J S T Fall, 3 Naval Squadron, Marieux, France, April 1917

Joe Fall was joint leading scorer with the Pup, and he claimed three victories with N6205 on 23 and 29 April and 1 May 1917. He had the name *BETTY* painted on its fuselage, and the fighter also featured a red cowling and wheel covers. As far as is known, all names worn by 'Naval 3' Pups were applied in red and edged with white. This 'C' Flight machine was damaged on 11 May, and following repairs it served in England. Later still it became 9901 and was assigned as a ship's Pup.

4

Pup N6179 of Flt Sub-Lts A W Carter and J J Malone, 3 Naval Squadron, Marieux, France, April 1917

This Pup joined 'Naval 3' in February and was allocated to 'B' Flight, where it was named *BABY MINE* – the aircraft later transferred to 'C' Flight. Flown by Flt Cdr T C Vernon and then Alfred Carter, it accounted for six German aircraft (three were credited to Carter). It displays a broad white band around the fuselage just aft of the fuselage roundel. Again, the front part of the cowling was be painted in the appropriate flight colour. This machine later served with the Seaplane Defence Flight at Dunkirk and a Home Defence squadron at Manston, in Kent.

5

Pup N6160 of Flt Cdr R Collishaw, 3 Naval Squadron, Bertangles, France, February 1917

Although more famous as a Sopwith Triplane and then a Camel ace, Ray Collishaw did claim two victories with this machine in February and March 1917. A W Carter also scored his first victory with it on 6 April. The Pup is shown as it appeared at Dunkirk just prior to being transferred to 'Naval 3', whose markings have not been confirmed. On 23 April, H S Kerby was at the controls of N6160 when he observed two Albatros D IIIs collide while under his attack. As an 'A' Flight machine, it would have carried the appropriate cowling identification of natural metal and then blue. Collishaw was in 'C' Flight, however, so whether or not he flew another flight's aircraft or N6160 changed flights is unclear. This Pup later served in England, surviving until May 1918 when 'Naval 9' Triplane veteran Capt J C Tanner was severally injured in a mid-air collision from which he later died.

6

Pup N6203 of Flt Cdr L H Slatter, Seaplane Defence Flight, Dunkirk, France, July 1917

This machine had previously served with 'Naval 3', the latter unit's H S Broad claiming two victories with it in April 1917. Although it was not an 'ace' Pup, N6203 was later flown by ace pilot Leonard Slatter. It is an interestingly marked machine, displaying the name *MINA* on both sides of the fuselage in black, edged in white, and a large 'S' on the fuselage decking – presumably S for Slatter. It was also adorned with two tear-shaped markings on the tailplane. The Pup went on to serve with 'Naval 12', and later flew a series of experimental flights from Grain. It was still on active duty in mid-1918.

7

Pup N6200 of Flt Cdr A M Shook, 4 Naval Squadron, Bray Dunes, France, May 1917

Shook claimed all three of his Pup victories in this 'B' Flight machine, which he named *BOBS*. On the morning of 19 May 1917 N6200 suffered engine failure whilst Shook was patrolling over the sea, forcing him to ditch. The Pup was duly salvaged and brought ashore by a French destroyer. Once repaired, it flew home defence sorties, but N6200 suffered several more crashes and was taken off charge in March 1918.

8

Pup N9899 of Flt Sub-Lt A J Chadwick, 4 Naval Squadron, Bray Dunes, France, May 1917

Although officially the serial number of this Pup was simply 9899, at some stage an 'N' prefix was added to it possibly to make the fighter appear more 'naval'. It displays the name *DO-DO* painted in white letters on the fuselage. Prior to its service with 'Naval 4', the Scout had been flown by 'Naval 3's' future Pup ace Jimmy Glen, after which it briefly served with 'Naval 8'. Once it finally reached 'Naval 4', the well travelled fighter was issued to 'B' Flight's Arnold Chadwick, who claimed his first of five Pup victories with it on 26 April 1917. The aircraft was later flown by aces A J Enstone (who also scored a victory with it), G W Hemming (who claimed two) and

A M Shook. Re-allocated to 'Naval 11', the fighter claimed a fifth victory when Flt Sub-Lt H F Airey downed a two-seater on 16 July. The latter pilot subsequently wrote the aircraft off when he ran it into a ditch in August.

9

Pup N6183 of Flt Cdr J A Glen, 3 Naval Squadron, Marieux, France, May 1917

Jimmy Glen scored his first two victories while flying this machine on 23 and 27 May 1917, followed by two more (both seaplanes) on 7 July. He named N6183 *MILDRED H*, and it remained with 'Naval 3' until late July, when it was transferred to 'Naval 11'. The Scout was wrecked while serving with the latter unit the following month. N6183 has a metal engine cowling, the whole front portion of which is painted in the 'B' Flight colour of red. Its wheel covers appear to have been decorated with red, white and blue circles.

10

Pup B1703 of Capt J O Andrews, No 66 Sqn, Vert Galand, France, June 1917

John Andrews was already an ace on DH 2s by the time he became a flight commander with No 66 Sqn in early April 1917. He claimed a further five Pup victories, the last three of which came in this aircraft on 13 May, 7 June and 11 July. It has plain features, with the only identifying mark being a 'I' painted on the engine cowling, plus Andrews' flight leader's pennants flying from the wing struts. In all, B1703 was involved in five successful combats, with another terminating in a forced landing. It was finally struck off charge in August after being badly shot-up in combat on 27 July.

11

Pup A7309 of Capt P G Taylor, No 66 Sqn, Vert Galand, France, June 1917

The dust jacket of Sir Gordon Taylor's well-known book *Sopwith Scout 7309* features a painting of this Pup, and while the artwork looks basically fine, the serial number lacks its letter prefix 'A'. Although the Author has seen a photograph of another Pup without its prefix, it must be assumed that Taylor's machine would have shown it in full, which is how it is depicted here. The Scout was originally marked with a '2' if a captioned photo in his book is correct. A7309 was certainly later marked with an 'A' on the fuselage, along with the unit marking of a white line running horizontally along the middle of the fuselage sides, broken only by the roundel and the aircraft letter.

12

Pup B2162 of 2Lt W A Pritt, No 66 Sqn, Estrée-Blanche, France, September 1917

This machine served with No 66 Sqn during the summer of 1917, arriving in July and being flown by W A Pritt. It is coded with the aircraft letter 'N', painted aft of the fuselage roundel and over the white fuselage squadron identification stripe. Its wheel covers were possibly divided in alternate segments of white and blue. Unusually, the Scout boasted a Lewis gun on its top wing in addition to the standard Vickers 0.303-in weapon mounted on the engine cowling. After his final combat success on 30 September, Pritt crashed in this machine and it was struck off charge five days later.

13

Pup A7327 of Capt S H Pratt, No 46 Sqn, La Gorgue, France, June 1917

This well-known Pup displays some interesting markings. The individual identification number '1' on the fuselage aft of the roundel was repeated twice on the top wing just inboard of the two roundels. Pratt had also painted a skull and crossbones motif in white on the top wing centre section, which was repeated on both wheel covers, the white paint showing up well against the red-doped canvas. The serial number was painted on the tailfin in black, edged white. The cowling was unpainted natural metal. Pratt led 'C' Flight, and he claimed all five of his Pup victories in A7327 between 25 May and 17 June 1917.

14

Pup B1777 of Capt A S G Lee, No 46 Sqn, Ste-Marie-Capel, France, September 1917

The colourful markings of this Pup were applied while the squadron was based at Suttons Farm, Essex, in July–August 1917 during one of the Gotha scares. Arthur Gould Lee had the name *CHIN-CHOW* painted beneath the cockpit as a reference to a character in a popular London west-end show of the time. The wheel covers were red, there was a red circle on the top wing centre section and a white '4' on the fuselage aft of the roundel, which was repeated twice on the top wing. Being a presentation aircraft, it also has *BRITISH GUIANA Nº 2* painted in white just above the name. Lee's personal markings were removed from the Pup shortly after No 46 Sqn's return to France on 30 August, B1777 becoming aircraft 'X', although the presentation name remained. In all, Lee scored five victories with this Pup between 4 and 30 September 1917.

15

Pup B1802 of Lt C W Odell, No 46 Sqn, Izel-le-Hameau, France, September 1917

Arriving at the squadron while it was based at Suttons Farm, B1802 was named *Will of the Wisp* and coded with the letter 'W' in white aft of the fuselage roundel. It is unclear where the name was painted, but in any event it may well have been deleted once the unit returned to France. The Pup displays two vertical white fuselage bands forward of the tail, which helps date a photo of B1802, as these markings were not allocated until after 19 September. Odell was flying this aircraft when he shared in the destruction of a two-seater on 24 September. Six days later the Pup was badly shot up in combat to the extent that its pilot, 2Lt E Armitage, later died of his wounds.

16

Pup A6156 of Capt O Stewart, No 54 Sqn, Flez, France, May 1917

Oliver Stewart claimed three German aircraft while flying this machine between April and June 1917. He personalised it with a monogram of his initials on the fuselage just forward of the roundel, this marking being repeated on the top wing centre section. Two other pilots claimed a victory while flying it, so A6156 was involved in five successful combats. Stewart displayed his monogram on subsequent Pups. There is a photograph on page 48 of this book showing a *III* after the monogram, so it may be assumed that this was his third such Pup so-marked. Stewart claimed two victories in A6211, but it has not been confirmed if this was *II* or *III*.

INDEX

Figures in **bold** refer to illustrations. Colour plates are shown as plate number(s) with caption locators in brackets.